From Strength to Strength

From

Strength

to

Strength

※

FINDING SUCCESS, HAPPINESS, AND
DEEP PURPOSE IN THE SECOND HALF OF LIFE

Arthur C. Brooks

PORTFOLIO / PENGUIN

Portfolio / Penguin
An imprint of Penguin Random House LLC
penguinrandomhouse.com

Most Portfolio books are available at a discount when purchased in quantity for sales
promotions or corporate use. Special editions, which include personalized covers,
excerpts, and corporate imprints, can be created when purchased in large quantities. For
more information, please call (212) 572-2232 or e-mail specialmarkets @ penguin
randomhouse.com. Your local bookstore can also assist with discounted bulk purchases
using the Penguin Random House corporate Business-to-Business program. For
assistance in locating a participating retailer, e-mail B2B@penguinrandomhouse.com.

Grateful acknowledgment is made for permission to reprint "I'm Nobody! Who are you?"
excerpted from *The Poems of Emily Dickinson: Variorum Edition,* edited by Ralph W.
Franklin, Cambridge, Mass.: The Belknap Press of Harvard University Press, Copyright
© 1998 by the President and Fellows of Harvard College. Copyright © 1951, 1955 by the
President and Fellows of Harvard College. Copyright © renewed 1979, 1983 by the
President and Fellows of Harvard College. Copyright © 1914, 1918, 1919, 1924, 1929, 1930,
1932, 1935, 1937, 1942 by Martha Dickinson Bianchi. Copyright © 1952, 1957, 1958,
1963, 1965 by Mary L. Hampson. Used by permission. All rights reserved.

Library of Congress Cataloging-in-Publication Data
Names: Brooks, Arthur C., 1964– author.
Title: From strength to strength: finding success, happiness, and deep purpose
in the second half of life / Arthur C. Brooks.
Description: First Edition. | New York: Portfolio/Penguin, 2022. |
Includes bibliographical references and index.
Identifiers: LCCN 2021040786 (print) | LCCN 2021040787 (ebook) |
ISBN 9780593191484 (hardcover) | ISBN 9780593191491 (ebook)
Subjects: LCSH: Older people—Psychology. | Aging—Psychological aspects. |
Spirituality. | Happiness.
Classification: LCC BF724.8 .B76 2022 (print) |
LCC BF724.8 (ebook) | DDC 155.67–dc23/eng/20211015
LC record available at https://lccn.loc.gov/2021040786
LC ebook record available at https://lccn.loc.gov/2021040787

Printed in the United States of America
4th Printing

Book design by Jennifer Daddio / Bookmark Design & Media

Some names and identifying characteristics have been changed
to protect the privacy of the individuals involved.

While the author has made every effort to provide accurate internet addresses at the time of
publication, neither the publisher nor the author assumes any responsibility for errors or for
changes that occur after publication. Further, the publisher does not have any control over
and does not assume any responsibility for author or third-party websites or their content.

To my guru

Blessed are those whose strength is in you,

whose hearts are set on pilgrimage.

As they pass through the Valley of Baka,

they make it a place of springs;

the autumn rains also cover it with pools.

They go from strength to strength,

till each appears before God in Zion.

PSALM 84: 5–7

Contents

The Man
on the Plane
Who Changed
My Life

"It's not true that no one needs you anymore."

These exasperated words came from an elderly woman sitting behind me on a late-night flight from Los Angeles to Washington, DC. The plane was dark and quiet, and most people were either sleeping or watching a movie. I was working on my laptop, feverishly trying to finish something now completely lost to memory but that at the time seemed to be of crucial importance to my life, happiness, and future.

A man I assumed to be her husband murmured almost inaudibly in response.

Again, his wife: "Oh, stop saying it would be better if you were dead."

Now they had my full attention. I didn't mean to eavesdrop but couldn't help it. I listened half with human empathy and half with the professional fascination of a social scientist. I formed an image of the husband in my head. I imagined someone who had worked hard all his life in relative obscurity; someone disappointed at his dreams unfulfilled—perhaps the career he never pursued, the schools he never attended, the company he never started. Now, I imagined, he was forced to retire, tossed aside like yesterday's news.

As the lights switched on after touchdown, I finally got a look at the desolate man. I was shocked: I recognized him—he was well-known; famous, even. Then in his mideighties, he has been universally beloved as a hero for his courage, patriotism, and accomplishments of many decades ago. I have admired him since I was young.

As he passed up the aisle of the plane behind me, passengers recognized him and murmured with veneration. Standing at the door of the cockpit, the pilot recognized him and said, echoing my own thoughts, "Sir, I have admired you since I was a little boy." The older man—apparently wishing for death just a few minutes earlier—beamed at the recognition of his past glories.

I wondered: Which more accurately describes the man—the one filled with joy and pride right now, or the one twenty minutes ago, telling his wife he might as well be dead?

I COULDN'T GET the cognitive dissonance of that scene out of my mind over the following weeks.

It was the summer of 2012, shortly after my forty-eighth birthday. I was not world-famous like the man on the plane, but my professional life was going pretty well. I was the president of a prominent Washington, DC, think tank that was prospering. I had written some bestselling books. People came to my speeches. My columns were published in *The New York Times*.

I had found a list written on my fortieth birthday, eight years earlier, of my professional goals—those that, if accomplished, would (I was sure) bring me satisfaction. I had met or exceeded all of them. And yet . . . I wasn't particularly satisfied or happy. I had gotten my heart's desire, at least as I imagined it, but it didn't bring the joy I envisioned.

And even if it *did* deliver satisfaction, could I really keep this going? If I stayed at it seven days a week, twelve hours a day—which I basically did, with my eighty-hour workweeks—at some point my progress would slow and stop. Many days I was thinking this flowing had already started. And what then? Would I wind up looking back on my life and telling my long-suffering wife, Ester, that *I* might as well be dead? Was there any way to get off the hamster wheel of success and accept inevitable professional decline with grace? Maybe even turn it into opportunity?

THOUGH THESE QUESTIONS WERE PERSONAL, I decided to approach them as the social scientist I am, treating them as a research project. It felt unnatural—like a surgeon taking out his own appendix. I plunged ahead, however, and for the last nine years I have been on a personal quest to turn my future from a matter of dread to an opportunity for progress.

I delved into divergent literatures, from my own field in social science to adjacent work in brain science, philosophy, theology, and history. I dug into the biographies of some of the most successful people in history. I immersed myself in the research on people who strive for excellence and interviewed hundreds of leaders, from heads of state to hardware-store owners.

What I found was a hidden source of anguish that wasn't just widespread but nearly universal among people who have done well in their careers. I came to call this the "striver's curse": people who strive to be excellent at what they do often wind up finding their inevitable decline terrifying, their successes increasingly unsatisfying, and their relationships lacking.

The good news is that I also discovered what I was looking for: a way to escape the curse. Methodically, I built a strategic plan for the rest of my life, giving me the chance to have a second half of adulthood that is not only not disappointing but happier and more meaningful than the first.

But I quickly realized that creating a private life plan wasn't good enough. I had to share it. The secrets I found were available to anyone with a will to live a life of joy and purpose—and willing to do the work to achieve it. Unlike the world we have tried to conquer earlier in life, here there was no competition for the prizes. We can all succeed and all be happier. And that is why I have written this book for you, my fellow striver.

The fact that you picked up this book tells me you have most likely achieved success through hard work, huge sacrifice, and uncompromising excellence. (And let's be honest—probably no small amount of good luck, too.) You deserve a lot of praise and admiration, and you've probably gotten it. But you know intellectually that you can't keep this party going forever, and you might even already see the signs that it is coming to an end. Unfortunately, you never gave much thought to the party's end, so you only really have one strategy: Try to keep it going. Deny change and work harder.

But that is a sure path to misery. In my field of economics, we have something called "Stein's law," named after the famous economist Herbert Stein from the 1970s: "If something cannot go on forever, it will stop."[1] Obvious, right? Well, when it comes to their own lives, people ignore it all the time. But you ignore this about your professional success at your peril. It will leave you falling further and further behind, shaking your fist at the heavens.

There is another path, though: Instead of denying change in your abilities, you can make the change itself a source of strength. Instead of trying to avoid decline, you can transcend it by finding a *new* kind of success, better than what the world promises and not a source of neurosis and addiction; a *deeper* form of happiness than what you had before; and, in the process, *true* meaning in life—maybe for the first time. The process is what I lay out in this book. It has changed my life, and it can change yours, too.

A word of caution, though: This path means going against many of your striverly instincts. I'm going to ask you not to deny your weaknesses but rather to embrace them defenselessly. To let go of some things in your life that you worked hard for—but that are now holding you back. To adopt parts of life that will make you happy, even if they don't make you *special*. To face decline—and even death—with courage and confidence. To rebuild the relationships you neglected on the long road to worldly success. And to dive into the uncertainty of a transition you have worked so hard to evade.

None of this is easy—it's hard to teach an old striver new tricks! It takes great effort to accept ideas that might have seemed crazy when you were doing everything under your power to be truly great at your worldly vocation. But I promise you the payoff will be worth it. I—and you—can get happier every year.

We can go from strength to strength.

From Strength to Strength

CHAPTER 1

Your Professional Decline Is Coming (Much) Sooner Than You Think

Who are the five greatest scientists who have ever lived? This is the kind of question people like to debate in nerdy corners of the internet that you probably don't visit, and I don't intend to take you there. But no matter how much or little you know about science, your list is sure to contain Charles Darwin. He is remembered today as a man who changed our understanding of biology completely and permanently. So profound was his influence that his celebrity has never wavered since his death in 1882.

And yet Darwin died considering his career to be a disappointment.

Let's back up. Darwin's parents wanted him to be a clergy-
man, a career for which he had little enthusiasm or aptitude.
As such, he was a lackluster student. His true love was science,
which made him feel happy and alive. So it was the opportunity
of a lifetime to him—"by far the most important event in my
life," he later called it—when, in 1831 at age twenty-two, he was
invited to join the voyage of *The Beagle*, a scientific sailing in-
vestigation around the world. For the next five years aboard the
ship, he collected exotic plant and animal samples, sending
them back to England to the fascination of scientists and the
general public.

This was impressive enough to make him pretty well-known.
When he returned home at age twenty-seven, however, he started
an intellectual fire with his theory of natural selection, the idea
that over generations, species change and adapt, giving us the
multiplicity of plants and animals we see after hundreds of
millions of years. Over the next thirty years, he developed his
theory and published it in books and essays, his reputation
growing steadily. In 1859, at age fifty, he published his mag-
num opus and crowning achievement, *On the Origin of Species*,
a bestseller explaining his theory of evolution that made him
into a household name and changed science forever.

At this point, however, Darwin's work stagnated creatively:
he hit a wall in his research and could not make new breakthroughs. Around that same time, a Czech monk by the name of
Gregor Mendel discovered what Darwin needed to continue his
work: the theory of genetics. Unfortunately, Mendel's work was
published in an obscure German academic journal and Darwin

never saw it—and in any case, Darwin (who, remember, had been an unmotivated student) did not have the mathematical or language skills to understand it. Despite his writing numerous books later in life, his work after that broke little ground.

In his last years, Darwin was still very famous—indeed, after his death he was buried as a national hero in Westminster Abbey—but he was increasingly unhappy about his life, seeing his work as unsatisfying, unsatisfactory, and unoriginal. "I have not the heart or strength at my age to begin any investigations lasting years, which is the only thing which I enjoy," he confessed to a friend. "I have everything to make me happy and contented, but life has become very wearisome to me."[1]

Darwin was successful by the world's standards, washed up by his own. He knew that by all worldly rights, he had everything to make him "happy and contented" but confessed that his fame and fortune were now like eating straw. Only progress and new successes such as he enjoyed in his past work could cheer him up—and this was now beyond his abilities. So he was consigned to unhappiness in his decline. Darwin's melancholy did not abate, by all accounts, before he died at seventy-three.

I'd like to be able to tell you that Darwin's decline and unhappiness in old age were as rare as his achievements, but that's not true. In fact, Darwin's decline was completely normal, and right on schedule. And if you, like Darwin, have worked hard to be exceptional at what you do, you will almost certainly face a similar pattern of decline and disappointment—and it will come much, much sooner than you think.

The surprising earliness of decline

Unless you follow the James Dean formula—"Live fast, die young, leave a good-looking corpse"—you know that your professional, physical, and mental decline is inevitable. You probably just think it's a long, long way off.

You're not alone in thinking this. For most people, the implicit belief is that aging and its effect on professional performance are something that happen far in the future. This attitude explains all kinds of funny survey results. For example, when asked in 2009 what "being old" means, the most popular response among Americans was "turning eighty-five."[2] In other words, the average American (who lives to seventy-nine) dies six years before entering old age.

Here is the reality: in practically every high-skill profession, decline sets in sometime between one's late thirties and early fifties. Sorry, I know that stings. And it gets worse: the more accomplished one is at the peak of one's career, the more pronounced decline seems once it has set in.

Obviously, you aren't just going to take my word for this, so let's take a look at the evidence.

We'll start with the most obvious, and earliest, decline: athletes. Those playing sports requiring explosive power or sprinting see peak performance from twenty to twenty-seven years of age, while those playing endurance sports peak a bit later—but still as young adults.[3] No surprise there—no one expects a serious athlete to remain competitive until age sixty, and most of the athletes I talked to for this book (there aren't any surveys asking when people expect to experience their physical decline, so I started doing so informally) figured they would have to find a new line of work by the time they were thirty. They don't love this reality, but they generally face it.

It's a much different story for what we now call "knowledge workers"—most people reading this book, I would guess. Among people in professions requiring ideas and intellect rather than athletic skill and significant physical strength, almost no one admits expecting decline before their seventies; some later than that. Unlike athletes, however, they are *not* facing reality.

Take scientists. Benjamin Jones, a professor of strategy and entrepreneurship at the Kellogg School of Management at Northwestern University, has spent years studying when people are most likely to make prizewinning scientific discoveries and key inventions. Looking at major inventors and Nobel winners going back more than a century, Jones finds that the most common age for great discovery is one's late thirties. He shows that the likelihood of a major discovery increases steadily through one's twenties and thirties and then declines dramatically through one's forties, fifties, and sixties. There are outliers, of course. But the probability of producing a major innovation at age seventy is approximately equal to what it was at age twenty—about zero.[4]

That fact no doubt inspired Paul Dirac, the Nobel Prize-winning physicist, to pen a little melancholy verse about how age is every physicist's curse. It ends with these two lines:

He is better dead than living still
when once he is past his thirtieth year.

Dirac won the prize when he was thirty-one years old, for work he had done in his midtwenties. By his thirtieth birthday, he had developed a general theory of the quantum field, the area in which he had earned his PhD at Cambridge (at age twenty-four). At twenty-eight he wrote *The Principles of Quantum Mechanics*, a textbook still in use today. At thirty he was a chaired professor at Cambridge. And after that? He was an active scholar and made a few breakthroughs. But it was nothing like the early years. Hence his poem.

Of course, Nobel winners might be different than ordinary scientists. Jones, with a coauthor, dug deeper into the data on researchers in physics, chemistry, and medicine who had highly cited work, as well as patents and various prizes. They found that peak performance is occurring at later ages than in the past, principally because the knowledge required to do cutting-edge work has increased so much over the decades. Still, since 1985, the peak age is not old: for physicists, fifty; for chemistry, forty-six; and for medicine, forty-five. After that, innovation drops precipitously.

Other knowledge fields follow the same basic pattern. For writers, decline sets in between about forty and fifty-five.[5] Financial professionals reach peak performance between the ages of thirty-six and forty.[6] Or take doctors: they appear to peak in their thirties, with steep drop-offs in skill as the years pass.[7] It's sort of reassuring to have a doctor who reminds people my age of Marcus Welby, MD. However, one recent Canadian study looked at 80 percent of the country's anesthesiologists and patient litigation against them over a ten-year period. The researchers found that physicians over sixty-five are 50 percent more likely than younger doctors (under fifty-one) at being found at fault for malpractice.

Entrepreneurs are an interesting case when it comes to peak age. Tech founders often earn vast fame and fortune in their twenties but many are in creative decline by age thirty. The *Harvard Business Review* has reported that founders of enterprises backed with $1 billion or more in venture capital tend to cluster in the twenty to thirty-four age range. The number of founders older than this, they discovered, is low. Other scholars dispute this finding, claiming that the average age of the founders of the highest-growth start-ups is, in fact, forty-five.[8] But the point remains the same: by middle age, entrepreneurial ability is plummeting. Even by the most optimistic estimates, only about 5 percent of founders are over sixty.

The pattern isn't limited to knowledge work; noticeable age-related decline comes earlier than people think in skilled jobs from policing to nursing. Peak performance is thirty-five to forty-four for equipment-service engineers and office workers; it is forty-five to fifty-four for semiskilled assembly workers and mail sorters.[9] The age-related decline among air-traffic controllers is so sharp—and the consequences of decline-related errors so dire—that the mandatory retirement age is fifty-six.[10]

Decline is so predictable that one scholar has built an eerily accurate model to predict it in specific professions. Dean Keith Simonton from the University of California, Davis, studied the pattern of professional decline among people in creative professions and built a model that estimates the shape of the average person's career. Fitting curves to gigabytes of data, he created a graph that looks like figure 1.

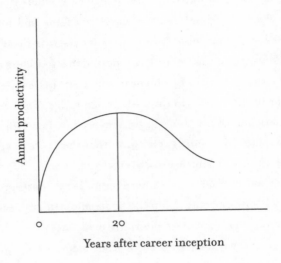

Figure 1. Average work productivity after career inception for creative and scholarly careers[11]

On average, the peak of creative careers occurs at about twenty years after career inception, hence the finding that people usually start declining somewhere between thirty-five and fifty. This is averaged across lots of fields, however, and Simonton found a fair amount of variation. For example, he has looked at the "half-life" of many professions—the age at which half of one's work has been produced. That would more or less correspond, on average, with the highest point in the graph. A group that closely tracks this twenty-year half-life is novelists, who generally do half their work before, and half after, 20.4 years from the start of their writing careers. Also close to this are mathematicians, who have a half-life of 21.7 years. Slightly earlier are poets, who hit their half-life after 15.4 years. Slightly later are geologists, at 28.9 years.

Let's think what this means for a moment. Say you are involved in a quantitative field—you are a data analyst, for example. If you finish your education and start your career at twenty-two, you will, on average, hit your professional peak at forty-four and then start to see your skills decline. Now say you are a poet—freshly minted with a master of fine arts degree at age twenty-five. Simonton's data show that you will burn through half your life's work by about age forty and be in productivity decline after that. On the other hand, if you are a geologist, your peak will tend to come closer to fifty-four.

For me, early decline is personal

When I started this research, I was especially keen to see if the decline patterns applied to musicians, especially classical musicians. There are some famous cases of classical musicians who go on and on, performing into old age. In 1945, double bass player Jane Little joined the Atlanta Symphony at the tender age of sixteen. She retired seventy-one years later at the age of eighty-seven. (Well, she didn't exactly retire: she actually died onstage during a concert while performing "There's No Business Like Show Business.")[12]

Ms. Little is not the norm, however; most retire much earlier.

And arguably, retirement happens too late. In surveys, classical musicians report that peak performance occurs in one's thirties. Younger players often groan over the prime spots occupied by older players with tenure—orchestras have tenure just like universities—who hang around long after they've lost their edge. The problem is, these older players often can't admit decline even to themselves. "It's very hard to admit that it's time," said one fifty-eight-year-old French horn player in the Pittsburgh Symphony Orchestra. "We're expert at denial. We have been successful because we refuse to accept the overwhelming odds at making it in our profession, so early in our development denial is a positive."[3]

That French horn player wasn't me. But it could have been, in a parallel life.

As a child, in fact, I had just one goal: to be the world's greatest French horn player. I practiced my horn slavishly, hours and hours a day, playing in any ensemble I could find. I had pictures of famous horn players on my bedroom wall for inspiration. I went to all the best music festivals and studied with the greatest teachers available to a lower-middle-class kid in Seattle. I was always the best player, the first chair.

For a while, I thought my young life's dream might come true. At nineteen, I left college to take a job playing professionally in a touring chamber-music ensemble. We played one hundred concerts a year, driving around the country in an oversized van. I didn't have health insurance and rent day was always nerve-wracking, but by the age of twenty-one I had seen all fifty states and fifteen foreign countries and made albums that occasionally I would hear on the radio. My dream was to rise through the classical-music ranks in my twenties, join a top symphony orchestra in a few years, and then become a soloist—the most exalted job a classical musician can hold.

But then, in my early twenties, a strange thing happened: I started getting worse. To this day, I have no idea why. My technique began to suffer, and I had no explanation for it. Nothing helped. I visited famous teachers and practiced more, but I couldn't get back to where I had been. Pieces that had been easy to play became hard; pieces that had been hard became impossible.

Perhaps the worst moment in my young but flailing career was at Carnegie Hall in New York City. While delivering a short speech about the music I was about to play, I stepped forward, lost my footing, and fell off the stage into the audience. On the way home from the concert, I mused darkly that the experience was surely a message from God.

Whether from God or not, I didn't listen to that message. I had no concept of myself apart from "great French horn player." I would rather have died than given up.

I sputtered along for nine more years. At twenty-five, I took a position in the City Orchestra of Barcelona, where I increased my practicing but my playing continued to deteriorate. After a few years, I found a job teaching at a small music conservatory in Florida, hoping for a magical turnaround that never materialized.

Realizing that maybe I ought to hedge my bets, without telling a soul but my wife (I felt ashamed) I went back to college via distance learning. I never met a professor or set foot in a classroom and earned my bachelor's degree in economics a month before my thirtieth birthday. For me, graduation day meant walking out to the mailbox in my slippers to pick up my diploma. On the envelope was prominently written DO NOT FOLD. It was folded.

I secretly continued my studies at night, earning a master's degree in economics a year later. I kept up my practicing and continued to make my living as a musician all the while, hoping against hope that I'd see a comeback in my skills.

It didn't happen. And so, at thirty-one, I admitted defeat: I was never going to turn around my faltering musical career. But what else to do with my life? I reluctantly went into the family business. My father was an academic; his father was an academic. I abandoned my musical aspirations and started a PhD.

Life goes on, right? Sort of. After finishing my studies, I became a university professor engaged in social science research and teaching—work I enjoyed a lot. But I still thought every day about my beloved first, and true, vocation. Even now, I regularly dream that I am onstage. I can hear the orchestra and see the audience. I am in the zone of blissful musical flow, playing better than ever . . . and I wake to remember that my childhood aspirations are now only phantasms.

In truth, I'm lucky. I now know that my decline was coming, and I just got it a decade or two earlier than is ordinarily the case. As such, I was able to accommodate it early enough that I could redirect my life into a new line of intellectual work. Still, to this day, the sting of that early decline makes these words difficult to write. I vowed to myself that it wouldn't ever happen to me again.

But of course, the data don't lie: it *will* happen again.

Why we decline, and how it affects us

For most people, decline is not just an unwelcome surprise; it is also a huge mystery. We learn early on that practice makes perfect; there is plenty of research telling us that mastery comes from ten thousand hours of work, or some really high number like that. In other words, life has a formula: the more you do something, the better at it you become.

But then you don't. Progress isn't a straight line upward, as figure 1 showed. So what explains the downward portion?

One early theory was that intelligence decreases with age. Researchers compared raw cognitive ability (IQ) across people of all ages and consistently found that young people do much better than older people. This led to the view that IQ falls as we age—and thus our abilities decline as well. However, this analysis was fundamentally flawed: it compared better educated people (who are generally younger) with those who grew up with fewer educational opportunities. Looking at individuals over time, researchers find that intelligence decreases are much less pronounced than the older studies showed.[14]

A better explanation involved structural changes in the brain—specifically, the changing performance of the prefrontal cortex (the part of the brain behind your forehead). This is the last part of the brain to develop in childhood and first to exhibit decline in adulthood. It is primarily responsible for working memory, executive function, and inhibitory mechanisms—that is, the ability to block out information extraneous to the task at hand, so we can focus and improve in our core skill. A big, strong prefrontal cortex makes it possible for you to get better and better at your specialty, whether it is making a legal case, doing surgery, or driving a bus.

In middle age, the prefrontal cortex degrades in effectiveness, and this has several implications. The first is that rapid analysis and creative innovation will suffer—just what we would expect when looking at the evidence on decline.[15] The second is that some specific, once-easy skills become devilishly hard, like multitasking. Older people are much more easily distracted than younger people. If you have—or had—teenage kids, you might have found yourself telling them they can't study effectively while listening to music and texting their friends. Actually, it's *you* who can't do that. In fact, older adults can enhance their cognitive effectiveness precisely by taking their own advice: turn off the phone and music and go someplace completely quiet to think and work.[16]

Another skill is the recall of names and facts. By the time you are fifty, your brain is as crowded with information as the New York Public Library. Meanwhile, your personal research librarian is creaky, slow, and easily distracted. When you send him to get some information you need—say, someone's name—he takes a minute to stand up, stops for coffee, talks to an old friend in the periodicals, and then forgets where he was going in the first place.[17] Meanwhile, you are kicking yourself for forgetting something you have known for years. When the librarian finally shows back up and says, "That guy's name is Mike," Mike is long gone and you are doing something else.

Despite the annoyances, some people deal with decline fairly well. Take the case of Paul Dirac, the Nobel-winning physicist who wrote the sad little poem about physicists being washed up by age thirty. His most important work and most intensely productive years were indeed in his twenties and early thirties. After his midthirties, he was still an active scholar and did some good work, but not like before.

He made the best of it, though. In what can only be regarded as a work of late-in-life genius, at seventy, Dirac left dreary Cambridge and accepted a professorship at Florida State University. He spent his later years taking in the sun and swimming; at FSU each day he would eat lunch with colleagues and then take a nap. He did continue to publish papers—without any dramatic results. His last paper deals with a research question he was never able to answer and ends with these honest words: "I have spent many years searching . . . and have not yet found it. I shall continue to work on it as long as I can, and other people, I hope, will follow along such lines."[18]

Unfortunately, his equanimity is the exception to the rule. Take the case of Linus Pauling, the only individual to win two different Nobel Prizes in distinct fields. Like Dirac and so many others, his greatest insights came in his twenties. In his thirties he wrote his most famous book, *The Nature of the Chemical Bond*, which summarized his work from the previous decade. He won the Nobel Prize in Chemistry in 1954 for his work on chemical bonds, which he had done decades earlier.

Pauling continued to do research in science after his great discoveries but began to spend more time on public activism in, some believe, an effort to stay in the limelight. After World

War II, Pauling turned his attention to antinuclear crusading. As a Nobel-winning chemist and contemporary of the scientists who developed the atomic bomb, the anti-war movement in the United States and Europe elevated him to a position of major prominence.

Pauling was awarded a Nobel Peace Prize in 1962 for his work to abolish nuclear testing during the height of the Cold War. For obvious reasons, this made him a controversial political figure: to some he was a hero; to others, a scoundrel. The latter group highlighted the fact that he also won—and accepted—the Lenin Peace Prize from the Soviet Union in 1970.

Pauling's hunger for relevance then led him to promote faddish, quasi-scientific ideas. He promoted eugenics, believing that people with certain genetic conditions, such as sickle-cell disease, should be prominently tattooed as a warning to potential mates. More famously, he became obsessed with his own theory that vitamins could cure a host of diseases, even cancer, and massively extend life. He promoted what he called "orthomolecular psychiatry" to treat mentally ill patients with massive doses of vitamins.

Most likely, you have been told that high doses of vitamin C can prevent colds; this theory comes from Pauling's famous writings from the 1970s, which have been scientifically debunked many times, as were virtually all of his later ideas. Indeed, as Cambridge professor Stephen Cave documents, Pauling came to be known as something of a quack in mainstream medical circles and spent a good deal of the last decades of his life bitterly denouncing his many critics in science journals.[19]

The agony of irrelevance

I have no doubt that what made decline so hard for Pauling was that as his abilities declined, so did his relevance to the public. And whether we are famous or not, almost nothing feels worse than becoming irrelevant, or even useless, to others who once held us in esteem. I have heard this lament again and again as I did research for this book. For example, I talked to a rare-book dealer in New York. He loved his profession and enjoyed his career. But now . . . well, I'll let him speak for himself.

> I've been a rare-book dealer for my entire life; in
> business by twenty-four. I've been blessed—Bob Dylan,
> John Updike, J. M. Coetzee, Woodward and Bernstein,
> endless estates—Waugh, Pound, Churchill, Roosevelt.
> Twenty years ago at a dinner party folks would hang on
> what I had to say, anecdotes of travel in search of textual
> treasures, dealmaking. But over the last dozen years, I've
> seen myself through the eyes of the people across the
> table. What do they see? I guess I'd have to say " yesterday."

I spoke to a fifty-year-old woman working in a high-responsibility administrative post at a major university.

> If they ever refine software enough to reduce human
> error to the point where human eyeballs are no longer
> needed to double-check the work, I'm out of a job. I figure

I've got about five to ten years left. . . . I do try to hide my
decline, for the time being, while I'm at work, even
though I know I can't hide it forever. I want time enough
to make changes without losing my income, but if I get
fired one day, oh well. Life goes on, or it doesn't.

Or consider this, from a prominent female journalist in her
fifties:

Many days I lack motivation to dive into another ten
hours of very hard work. The cost of lost sleep or too
much travel takes a toll on our bodies. We used to
rebound quickly. Not anymore. The true decline
happened a lot to my colleagues in their forties. From my
outsider's view it looked like a weariness had set in.
Trudging out the door to another city council meeting/
highway crash/murder/tax story—all things they had
done one hundred times over the years. They were tired.

In 2007, a team of academic researchers at the University
of California, Los Angeles, and Princeton University analyzed
data on more than a thousand elderly people. Their findings,
published in the *Journal of Gerontology*, showed that senior citizens who never or rarely "felt useful" were nearly three times
as likely as those who frequently felt useful to develop a mild
disability and more than three times as likely to have died
during the course of the study.

You might reply that memories of past relevance should
be enough for us. That is a common assumption people make

as they try to accumulate a lot of money, power, and prestige—
that they can "make it" once and for all. Life is a treasure hunt,
this thinking goes—go out and find the pot of gold, and then you
can enjoy it and be happy for the rest of your life, even after
your glory days are past. Go get rich and retire early. Go get
famous and bask in the experience after it is past. In my profession, go earn tenure and you will be all set. Then, when
the success wanes, you can enjoy the memory of what you accomplished.

By this standard, the man on the plane I wrote about in the
introduction should have been the happiest guy in the world. He
was rich, famous, and respected for what he had done long ago.
He had won the race! The same goes for Darwin and Pauling.
But they *weren't* happy, because that model is all wrong. It is
based on a completely misbegotten model of human striving.
In fact, had the man on the plane had an "ordinary" life—had he
never accomplished something extraordinary—he might not
have felt so miserably irrelevant today.

We might call this the "principle of psychoprofessional gravitation": the idea that the agony of decline is directly related
to prestige previously achieved, and to one's emotional attachment to that prestige.[20] If you have low expectations and never
do much (or do a lot but maintain a Buddha-like level of non-
attachment to your professional prestige), you probably won't
suffer much when you decline. But if you attain excellence and
are deeply invested in it, you can feel pretty irrelevant when
you inevitably fall from those heights. And that is agony.

Great gifts and achievements early in life are simply not an
insurance policy against suffering later on. On the contrary,

studies show that people who have chased power and achievement in their professional lives tend to be unhappier after retirement than people who did not.[21]

Even simply being identified early on as gifted can lead to problems, according to Carole and Charles Holahan, psychologists at the University of Texas at Austin.[22] They looked at hundreds of elderly people who had been publicly identified as highly gifted early in life. The Holahans' conclusion: "Learning at a younger age of membership in a study of intellectual giftedness was related to . . . less favorable psychological well-being at age eighty."

The Holahans' study may simply be showing that it's hard to live up to high expectations, and that telling your kid she is a genius is pretty bad parenting. However, there is also evidence that high accomplishment affects people negatively when it finishes. Consider the case of professional athletes, many of whom struggle greatly after leaving their sports careers. Tragic examples abound, involving addiction or suicide; unhappiness in retired athletes may even be the norm, at least temporarily. I asked 1996 Olympic gold medal gymnast Dominique Dawes about how life feels after competing and winning at the highest levels. She told me that she enjoyed her normal life, but the adjustment wasn't easy, and still isn't. "My Olympic self will ruin my marriage and will leave my kids feeling inadequate," she told me bluntly. "Living life as if every day is an Olympics only makes those around me miserable." Dawes's post-Olympic life has been specifically engineered to avoid the pitfalls people face after ultra-high achievement; she has a good marriage, kids, and is very serious about her Catholic faith. She doesn't live in the past. Many other stars have not fared so well.

The fact that we can't store up our glories and enjoy them when they are long past gets to the problem of *dissatisfaction*—a problem we will confront later in this book. Humans simply aren't wired to enjoy an achievement long past. It is as if we were on a moving treadmill; satisfaction from success lasts but an instant. We can't stop to enjoy it; if we do, we zip off the back of the treadmill and wipe out. So we run and run, hoping that the next success, greater than the last, will bring the enduring satisfaction we crave.

The decline problem is a double whammy, then: we need ever-greater success to avoid dissatisfaction, yet our abilities to stay even are declining. No, it's actually a triple whammy, because as we try to stay even, we wind up in patterns of addictive behavior such as workaholism, which puts strivers into unhealthy relationship patterns at the cost of deep connection to spouses, children, and friends. By the time the wipeout occurs, there's no one there to help us get up and dust off.

That leads many achievers into a vicious cycle: terrified of decline, dissatisfied with victories that come less and less frequently, hooked on the successes that are increasingly of the past, and isolated from others. And it's not as if the world is overflowing with resources to help you. No one feels sorry for a successful person. The suffering of a striver with a comfortable life invokes the image of the world's smallest violin.

And yet it is real.

Where we go from here

Here is the bottom line, fellow striver: when it comes to the enviable skills that you worked so hard to attain and that made you successful in your field, you can expect significant decline to come as soon as your thirties, or as late as your early fifties. That's the deal, and it's not fun. Sorry.

So what are you going to do about it? There are really only three doors you can go through here:

1. You can deny the facts and rage against decline—setting yourself up for frustration and disappointment.
2. You can shrug and give in to decline—and experience your aging as an unavoidable tragedy.
3. You can accept that what got you to this point won't work to get you into the future—that you need to build some new strengths and skills.

If you choose door number 3, congratulations. There's a bright future ahead. But it requires a bunch of new skills and a new way of thinking.

CHAPTER 2

The Second Curve

DECLINE IS UNAVOIDABLE. Period. But aging isn't all bad news (and I'm not talking about grandkids and a condo in Sarasota, although that's got to be nice, too). In fact, there are some specific ways in which we naturally get smarter and more skillful. The trick to improving as we age is to understand, develop, and practice these new strengths. If you can—and I am going to show you how, don't worry—you can transform decline into incredible new success.

Did you ever notice that as people get old, they almost never become less articulate? They tend to have a richer vocabulary than they did earlier in life. This leads to a number of abilities. They are better Scrabble players, for example, and can do quite well in foreign languages—not in getting the accent perfect but in building vocabulary and understanding grammar. Studies bear out these observations: people maintain and grow their vocabulary—in their native languages and foreign languages—all the way to the end of life.[1]

Similarly, you may notice that with age, people are better at combining and utilizing complex ideas.[2] In other words, they may not be able to come up with shiny new inventions or solve problems quickly like in the old days. But they get much better at using the concepts they know and expressing them to others. They also get better at interpreting the ideas that others have—sometimes even to the people who came up with them.

I have found this in my life. I lived in Spain in my youth and have gone back and forth to Barcelona for more than thirty years. There are two languages in Barcelona—Spanish and Catalan—which I spoke well when I lived there, but which got a little rusty when I was living in the United States. Weirdly, I found that my ability in both improved starting around age fifty and is now better than it was even when I lived there. Similarly, as a social scientist, I am better at telling a story from data than I was earlier in my career. While I doubt I could write the scholarly papers I once did—sometimes I have trouble understanding the math in my own research from twenty years ago—I can tell you how insights relate to one another and how to apply them in your life. Hence, I am writing this book and not an impenetrable mathematical academic article. I invented ideas early on; I synthesize ideas—mine and others—now.

These abilities that appear later in life favor some specific professions. For example, theoretical mathematicians tend to peak and decline early, just as Simonton's data predict. But applied mathematicians (who use mathematics to, for example, solve actual problems in business) peak much later, because they specialize in combining and using ideas that already exist—a skill that favors older people. Or take historians, the quintessential assemblers of existing facts and ideas. Weirdly, they fall way out of the typical range for decline, peaking 39.7 years after career inception, on average. Think what this implies: Say you intend to pursue a career as a professional historian and finish your PhD at thirty-two. The bad news is that in your fifties, you are still pretty wet behind the ears. But here's the good news: at age seventy-two, you still have half your work to go! Better take care of your health so you can write your best books into your eighties.

If you take these facts as being random, you get very little actionable strategy for life, beyond perhaps becoming a competitive Scrabble player or working on a PhD in history. It isn't random, however—not at all. In the late 1960s, a British psychologist named Raymond Cattell set about finding an explanation for why all this happens.[3] He found the answer, and that answer can defeat the striver's curse—and change your life.

Two intelligences

In 1971, Cattell published a book entitled *Abilities: Their Structure, Growth, and Action.* In it, he posited that there were two types of intelligence that people possess, but at greater abundance at different points in life.

The first is *fluid intelligence*, which Cattell defined as the ability to reason, think flexibly, and solve novel problems. It is what we commonly think of as raw smarts, and researchers find that it is associated with both reading and mathematical ability.[4] Innovators typically have an abundance of fluid intelligence. Cattell, who specialized in intelligence testing, observed that it was highest relatively early in adulthood and diminished rapidly starting in one's thirties and forties.[5]

Based on this finding, Cattell believed younger people are naturally the best innovators in raw, new ideas. If he were alive today (he died in 1998 at the ripe old age of ninety-two), he would read what I have written up to this point and say right away that the professional decline I've been talking about—the initial abilities that fade all too early—comes from the fluid intelligence that virtually all hardworking, successful people rely on early in their careers.

If you have experienced professional success in the early part of your career, and your job involved new ideas or solving hard problems—most people reading this book, I would bet—you have fluid intelligence (plus your hard work, maybe your parents, and good luck) to thank for it. The young killers in almost every modern industry rely on fluid intelligence. They learn quickly, focus hard on what matters, and devise solutions. Unfortunately, as we have seen in abundant detail, you generally can't maintain this as you age—which once again might well be why you are reading this book.

That's not the end of the story, however, and this is where Cattell's work matters. Fluid intelligence isn't the only kind—

there is also *crystallized intelligence*. This is defined as the ability to use a stock of knowledge learned in the past. Think once again about the metaphor of a vast library. But this time, instead of regretting how slow the librarian is, marvel at the size of the book collection your librarian is wandering around in, and the fact that he knows where to find a book, even if it takes him a while. Crystallized intelligence, relying as it does on a stock of knowledge, tends to increase with age through one's forties, fifties, and sixties—and does not diminish until quite late in life, if at all.

Cattell himself described the two intelligences in this way: "[Fluid intelligence] is conceptualized as the decontextualized ability to solve abstract problems, while crystallized intelligence represents a person's knowledge gained during life by acculturation and learning."[6] Translation: When you are young, you have raw smarts; when you are old, you have wisdom. When you are young, you can generate lots of facts; when you are old, you know what they mean and how to use them.

Let's break things down a bit. Cattell is telling us that the success curve in figure 1 from the last chapter is, for all intents and purposes, the fluid intelligence curve, which increases to one's midthirties or so and then declines through the forties and fifties. Meanwhile, there is another curve lurking behind it, the crystallized intelligence curve, that is increasing through middle and late adulthood. Figure 2 gives an idea of what this looks like.

This is a big finding for you and me—huge, actually. It says that if your career relies solely on fluid intelligence, it's true

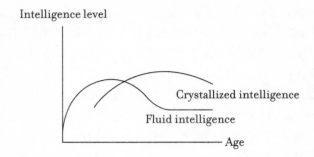

Figure 2. Fluid intelligence and crystallized intelligence curves

that you will peak and decline pretty early. But if your career requires crystallized intelligence—*or if you can repurpose your professional life to rely more on crystallized intelligence*—your peak will come later but your decline will happen much, much later, if ever. And if you can go from one type to the other—well, then you have cracked the code.

What about the career curves described earlier? In some cases, such as tech entrepreneurs, the career curve is effectively the same as that of fluid intelligence, which is why the fade happens at such a young age. Other fields, however, require an admixture of the two types of intelligence, placing the career high point somewhat later. And in some careers that rely almost entirely on a large mental library and ability to use it, the peak happens very late in life.

Almost without fail, you will notice the decline in the fluid intelligence portion. However, there always exists the ability to redesign your career less on *innovation* and more on *instruction* as the years pass, thus playing to your strengths with age. Some careers make this easier than others. The study of history, for example, is one career that requires huge stocks of knowledge and the wisdom to synthesize it; it is an almost pure crystallized intelligence field.

But there are other professions that are more common than being a historian. Notably, there is teaching, which once again requires verbal skill and a gift for explaining large amounts of accumulated information. No wonder this field favors the old over the young. A recent study in *The Chronicle of Higher Education* showed that the oldest college professors tended to have the best teaching evaluations within departments.[7] They found this especially in the humanities, where professors got their lowest ratings early in their careers and improved through their sixties and seventies. (A note to college students reading this book: enroll in the classes of the oldest professors.)

This late-in-life success probably partially explains the professional longevity of college professors, three quarters of whom plan to retire after age sixty-five (while the average retirement age in America is sixty-two).[8] I remember one day in my first year out of graduate school as an assistant professor, I struck up a conversation with a colleague in his late sixties. I asked him if he ever considered retiring. He laughed and told me he was more likely to leave his office horizontally than vertically.

Perhaps the dean would have chuckled ruefully at this comment—college administrators often complain that there is a noticeable drop-off in research productivity (which depends on fluid intelligence, especially for analytical work) among tenured faculty in the last decades of their careers. Older professors take up faculty lines that could otherwise be used to hire young scholars hungry to develop their research agendas (and who are overflowing with fluid intelligence). But therein lies an opportunity. The question is not how to stimulate older faculty to write more complicated academic journal articles; it is how to adjust their work portfolio toward teaching without loss of professional status.

The idea of moving to instruction later in life is a theme one finds in the great wisdom literatures from East to West. "Just as one uses a burning candle to light others with," says the elderly archery teacher in Eugen Herrigel's famous book *Zen in the Art of Archery*, "so the teacher transfers the spirit of the right art from heart to heart, that it may be illumined."

Or consider the wisdom of the first-century BC Roman statesman, lawyer, scholar, and philosopher Marcus Tullius Cicero. Cicero is the most important voice from that period that stills exists today: three quarters of the surviving Latin literature from Cicero's lifetime was written by him.[9] In his last year of life, he wrote an open letter to his son on the responsibilities of an upright person, entitled *De Officiis*. Much of it concerns the duties of a young person, but he also expounds on the vocation in the second half of life.

> The old . . . should, it seems, have their physical labors
> reduced; their mental activities should be actually
> increased. They should endeavor, too, by means of their
> counsel and practical wisdom to be of as much service as

possible to their friends and to the young, and above all to the state.[10]

Cicero believed three things about older age. First, that it should be dedicated to *service*, not goofing off. Second, our greatest gift later in life is *wisdom*, in which learning and thought create a worldview that can enrich others. Third, our natural ability at this point is *counsel*: mentoring, advising, and teaching others, in a way that does not amass worldly rewards of money, power, or prestige.

Cicero didn't just give good advice, by the way; he lived it—and died practicing it. He lived in a dangerous time for public intellectuals. We fret about cancel culture today; Cicero was *assassinated* at the age of sixty-three for his less than politically correct ideas (specifically, his criticism of Mark Antony after the murder of Julius Caesar). Running for his life due to his political views, he was captured by a Roman centurion and was about to be put to death. The pinnacle of crystallized intelligence, he was a teacher with his dying breath. "There is nothing proper about what you are doing, soldier," Cicero schooled the centurion. "But do try to kill me properly."[11]

The teaching gift of crystallized intelligence was on my mind a couple of years ago when I gave a speech to the employees of a prominent Silicon Valley tech firm. After my remarks, a young man in the audience asked me to weigh in on the diversity problem in his industry. He was referring to the lack of racial minorities and women in the engineering profession, and I was happy to address that point. But then I took the opportunity to ask whether anyone in his youth-dominated business ever thought about *age* diversity. "Do you have enough old people working here?" I asked. His response was instructive: "You mean people over thirty?" Punk.

The point is not to find jobs for the elderly; it is to glean the wisdom and experience from people who have seen a lot, have already made every stupid mistake in the book, and can teach the younger folks before they make avoidable errors. Over the last few years, the youth-dominated firms in the tech sector have been battered by scandals and plummeting public admiration. Where once they were venerated as the future of capitalism, today people often see their products as harmful and their leaders as selfish and childish. Older executives in other industries just shake their heads at the seemingly obvious mistakes the young tech entrepreneurs are making.

So what do the young hotshots need? Old people on product teams, old people in marketing, and old people in the C-suite. They need not just whiz-bang ideas but actual wisdom that only comes with years in the school of hard knocks.

The joys of the second curve

The existence of the second curve is great news for all of us. First, we now have an explanation for the typical drop-off in abilities in one's forties or fifties. In other words, if you are my age or older, *it isn't just you*. Second, there is a second wave to ride to success that favors people who are older. Third, by most estimations, what you get in this second wave is more valuable (if less lucrative and prestigious) than what you get in the first. After all, as the saying goes, "Knowledge is knowing that a tomato is a fruit; wisdom is knowing not to put it in a fruit salad."* Or more biblically, "Teach us to number our days, that we may gain a heart of wisdom."[12]

If you're experiencing decline in fluid intelligence—and if you are my age, *you are*—it doesn't mean you are washed up. It means it is time to jump off the fluid intelligence curve and onto the crystallized intelligence curve. Those who fight against time are trying to bend the old curve instead of getting onto the new one. But it is almost impossible to bend, which is why people are so frustrated, and usually unsuccessful.

So why do people try, over and over again? Two reasons: First, they are not aware that their first curve naturally bends down—they think something is wrong with *them*. And second, they don't know that another curve exists that will take them to a new kind of success.

And even if they do suspect there's another curve out there, it can be hard and scary to make the jump. It requires the courage and fortitude to make changes in our lives and careers—to become more of a teacher, whatever that means in one's specific field. Not everybody wants to do that. Many refuse.

But for those who make the jump, the reward is almost always enormous. In interviewing people for this book, I found that invariably, the people who are happiest and most satisfied in their fifties, sixties, and seventies are those who made this

---

* This aphorism has been credited to several different people over the years.

leap. Here are a couple of examples, starting with a fifty-eight-year-old male actuary. Here's what he told me:

> I am at the point in my career where I am looking forward to retirement, not as a chance to stop working but more as a chance to work on other things that I am finding have become very important to me. In addition to my day job I am teaching financial math one evening a week to graduate students. I find this very rewarding as I bring the insights of my long career to these young, aspiring minds. They have a thirst for learning and I enjoy meeting them and helping them see the insights beyond the textbooks.

A female television journalist told me something similar, after retiring to a teaching job at a small college:

> I feel lucky to be inside academia, which seems to value older people. I'm practically young compared to some of the faculty I work with and they are fascinating, brilliant folks. That's been one of the most wonderful differences between TV news and this. Adults are valued, hold leadership roles, and their knowledge is appreciated. Because TV news relies on innovation, this is not possible.

Be like Bach

In the last chapter, I gave some examples of prominent historical strivers—Charles Darwin, Linus Pauling—who either didn't know there was a second curve or simply couldn't make the jump. There are other examples from history of people who have done it spectacularly, however. My favorite example of involuntary decline followed by the joys of finding the second curve comes from the great composer Johann Sebastian Bach.

Born in 1685 to a long line of prominent musicians in central Germany, J. S. Bach quickly distinguished himself as a unique musical genius. In his lifetime he published more than a thousand compositions for all of the available instrumentations of his day.[13] The greatest cantatas for orchestra and chorus ever written seemed to fall off his pen by the dozens; his concerti are compositionally perfect; his piano works simple and elegant.

Bach is my favorite composer. I love his music so much that as a kid, I pointed out to people with pride that "Bach," translated into English, is the surname "Brook," or in its much more common form, "Brooks." Coincidence?

I am hardly unique in my love for Bach, though. The great twentieth-century Spanish cellist Pablo Casals, who brought Bach's suites for solo cello to a worldwide audience, said this of his musical hero: "To strip human nature until its divine attributes are made clear, to inform ordinary activities with spiritual fervor, to give wings of eternity to that which is most ephemeral; to make divine things human and human things divine; such is Bach, the greatest and purest moment in music of all time."[14]

Or, as the composer Robert Schumann put it, "Music owes as much to Bach as religion to its founder." I'm not sure I'd go so far as Schumann, comparing Bach to Jesus, but really—when you finish this chapter, go listen to his *Saint Matthew Passion* or Mass in B Minor, the piece I am listening to as I write these words. You will understand why some call him the "Fifth Evangelist."

Bach's prodigious output wasn't limited to music, by the way. He fathered twenty children, seven by his beloved first wife, Maria Barbara, who tragically died at thirty-five; thirteen more with his second wife, Anna Magdalena. Only ten of Bach's children lived to adulthood, but these included four composers who went on to attain significant fame in their own right. The greatest of these was Carl Philipp Emanuel, known as "C. P. E." to the generations that followed.[15]

J. S. Bach's musical vernacular was the high baroque. Early in his career he was considered by many to be the finest composer in this style ever to have lived. Commissions rolled in; royalty sought him out (specifically, Prince Leopold of Anhalt-Köthen); younger composers emulated his style. He lived in increasing prominence with his large, beloved family.

But his fame and glory didn't last—in no small part because his career was overtaken by musical events ushered in by a young up-and-comer who kicked him out of the limelight by rendering the high baroque as obsolete as disco. That usurper was none other than J. S.'s own son, C. P. E.

Early on, C. P. E. showed the same musical gifts his father had. As he developed, he mastered the baroque idiom but was more fascinated with a newfangled "classical" style of music that everyone wanted to hear. C. P. E.'s fame rose with the popularity of the classical style; meanwhile, baroque music became regarded as old-fashioned and stuffy, along with the composers—including J. S.—who would not, or could not, write in the new style.

And just like that, C. P. E. displaced J. S. as the family's musical celebrity.

For the last decades of J. S.'s life (and a century afterward), C. P. E. was considered the greatest of the Bachs. Joseph Haydn and Ludwig van Beethoven admired C. P. E. and collected his music. Wolfgang Amadeus Mozart himself said, "Bach is the father, we are the children," referring to C. P. E., *not* J. S.

J. S. Bach could easily have become embittered like Darwin, feeling left behind by the musical cognoscenti after a career at the forefront. Instead, he took pride in his son's originality and redesigned his own life, moving from musical innovator to master teacher. He spent the last ten years of his life working on, among other projects, *Die Kunst der Fuge—The Art of Fugue*—a collection of fugues and canons based on a single theme intended to teach the compositional techniques of the baroque.

The Art of Fugue was written as a kind of textbook. One hundred years after Bach's death, it was rediscovered and began to be performed in public. Today, it is common to hear it in concerts. Imagine a textbook so beautiful that it is considered a work of literature, or even poetry. That's the greatness of J. S. Bach. But just as impressive a feat as this was his personal resiliency. He experienced professional decline as a musical innovator. Far from frustration and depression, he finished out his life as a happy father and reinvented himself as a teacher.

J. S. died working on his master text—literally. The manuscript for his Contrapunctus 14 from *The Art of Fugue* stops midmeasure. None other than C. P. E. added these words some years later: "*Über dieser Fuge . . . ist der Verfasser gestorben*" ("At the point in the fugue . . . the composer died").[16] It also finished on a private joke for his family. Bach used this sequence of notes: Bb–A–C–B♮ in the fugue. In German notation, Bb is simply "B" and B♮ is "H." In other words, Bach was using B-A-C-H as a musical theme. And as fate would have it, these are the last notes he wrote. Strong finish.

Think back now on the life of Charles Darwin. On paper, the two great men are similar. Both were preternaturally gifted and attained fame for their early innovations and accomplishments. Both enjoyed tremendous respect even after their earlier innovations were overtaken by later events. And both attained permanent fame well after their deaths—J. S. Bach has eclipsed all other composers of his time (including C. P. E.) and is a popular favorite today even among casual listeners of serious music. Darwin is popularly known as one of the greatest scientists in history (while Gregor Mendel is unfamiliar to most people).

Where they differ is in the management of their own lives—in their approach to their midlife professional decline as *innovators*. When Darwin hit his wall, he became despondent and depressed; his life ended in sadness. Like most people, he never looked for or found his second curve, so all he saw late in life was his decline.

Meanwhile, when Bach saw the back half of his fluid intelligence curve, he jumped with both feet onto his crystallized intelligence curve and never looked back. When he fell behind as an innovator, he reinvented himself as an instructor. He died beloved, fulfilled, respected—if not as famous as he once had been—and, by all accounts, happy.

"Study Bach," said the great composer Johannes Brahms a century after Bach's death. "There you will find everything."[17] Because of his beautiful text *The Art of Fugue*, centuries of composers have been able to understand and re-create the techniques of the high baroque. He demonstrates the way to build a fugue or canon so clearly that any student can do it—not like the master, but in at least rudimentary fashion.

And so it is with his exemplary life, in which his calling was molded perfectly to his changing skills—and as such was filled with joy, love, and service to others. Let's take Brahms's advice not just for music, but study Bach to improve our lives as well.

We are all born with gifts. Some find them when they are young, like J. S. Bach, who made his mark as an adolescent, playing pieces on the organ at fifteen that others swore were impossible and going on to fame as a composer by his twenties. Some find their calling later, like so many of my students, who get their groove after many years of college and graduate school. Others find them only after realizing they were going in the wrong direction for a while, like a house builder I interviewed, who found his passion for building after completing a fancy education in science. Or like me—totally convinced that music was my calling until it was ripped from my grasp and I had to look elsewhere, finding it in the world of social science.

No matter how you find your passion, early on, pursue it with a white-hot flame, dedicating it to the good of the world. But hold your success lightly—be ready to change as your abilities change. Even if your worldly prestige falls, lean into the changes. Remember, every change of circumstances is a chance to learn, grow, and create value. This chapter shows that it is not a question of making the best of a bad situation; it is not missing out on a huge opportunity that only comes later in life.

J. S. Bach had no idea that his work as a teacher would be rediscovered a century after his death and played in concerts all over the world, rendering him the greatest composer in history in the eyes of millions. He simply thought he was using his gifts to greatest advantage, masterfully teaching what he loved and cheering the growing prestige of his children. Without knowing it, he jumped from one curve to the other.

Devote the back half of your life to serving others with your wisdom. Get old sharing the things you believe are most important. Excellence is always its own reward, and this is how you can be most excellent as you age.

Jumping onto the second curve

So here's the secret, fellow striver: Get on your second curve. Jump from what rewards fluid intelligence to what rewards crystallized intelligence. Learn to use your wisdom.

Obviously, I can't just leave it there. It's one thing to know that your next task is getting to that second curve. It's another to—*gulp*—actually jump off your first curve. That's hard, because it is precisely *not* what strivers do—they don't quit; they work harder. But you've seen the data, and they don't lie. Working harder doesn't work.

The rest of this book, therefore, is dedicated to helping you make the jump. First, I will show you the three forces holding you back, and how to remove them. They are your addiction to work and success, your attachment to worldly rewards, and your fear of decline. Then I'll show you the three things you need to do starting right now to make the second curve better than the first: develop your relationships, start your spiritual journey, and embrace your weaknesses. Finally, I'll tell you what you can expect to feel as you start your transition.

We are going to cover a lot of ground, but here's the short version: your second curve exists, you can get on it, and you will be very happy you did.

CHAPTER 3

Kick Your Success Addiction

PERHAPS THE MOST POIGNANT CONVERSATION I had when writing this book was with a woman about my age. She is tremendously successful on Wall Street—she's made a fortune and is highly respected.

Lately, however, she has been starting to miss a step here and there. Her decisions as a manager aren't as crisp as they once were, her instincts less reliable. Where once she commanded the room, now she sees that younger colleagues doubt her. In a panic about the prospect of decline, she read an article I wrote and reached out to me.

I asked her a lot of questions about her life. She wasn't very happy and hadn't been happy for many years—perhaps ever.

Her marriage was unsatisfactory, she drank a little too much, and her relationship with her college-age kids was all right . . . but distant. She had few *real* friends. She worked incredibly long hours and felt physically exhausted a lot of the time. Her work was everything to her—she "lived to work"—and now she was terrified that even *that* was starting to slip.

She openly admitted these things, so you'd think that the solution to her unhappiness would be obvious. And indeed, I asked her why she didn't remediate the sources of her unhappiness—to take the time to resuscitate her marriage and spend more time with her kids; get some help with her drinking; sleep more; get in better shape. I knew that her grueling work effort had made her successful in the first place, but when you figure out something has secondary consequences that are making you miserable, you find a way to fix it, right? You might love bread, but if you become gluten intolerant, you stop eating it because it makes you sick.

She thought about my question for a couple of minutes. Finally, she looked at me and said, matter-of-factly, "Maybe I would prefer to be *special* rather than *happy*."

Looking at my astonished face, she explained: "Anyone can do the things it takes to be happy—go on vacation, spend time with friends and family . . . but not everyone can accomplish great things." I initially scoffed at this but then thought about it in the privacy of my own mind. And I realized that I have also made this choice at points in my life. Maybe even most of the time, if I am honest with myself.

The financier had spent many years creating a version of herself that others would admire—including some who were dead, like her parents. More important, her curated self was a person *she* would admire—a hugely successful, hardworking executive. And she succeeded! But nothing is permanent, and now she felt like every hour of work was giving her less than the last, and not just less happiness—less power and prestige, too. Her problem was that the "special one" she had created was less than a full person. She had traded herself for a symbol of herself, you might say.

We too often do this to other people: reduce them to one or two enviable characteristics such as physical beauty, money, or power. This is called "objectification." Celebrities often talk about how terrible it is to be objectified in this way. Marriages based on objectification—marrying for money, for example— inevitably fail miserably.

We know in our hearts that the objectification of others is wrong and immoral. But it is easy to forget that we can do it to ourselves as well. My financier friend had objectified herself to be special, with a self-definition that revolved around work, achievement, worldly rewards, and pride. Even though that object was slowly eroding, she was too attached to her worldly success to make the changes that could now bring her happiness.

She was addicted—to work and, underneath that, to success. Like all addictions, these dehumanized her. She saw herself not as a full person but rather more like a high-performance machine—or perhaps one that used to be high performance but was now showing wear and tear.

Maybe you can relate to this. I can. In this chapter, we will get to the bottom of these problems—self-objectification, work- aholism, and, most of all, success addiction—that chain us to our declining fluid intelligence curve. But more important, we will see how to escape these tyrannies so we can make the jump to new success.

Hooked

"Maybe I would prefer to be *special* rather than *happy*."

The financier's words vaguely reminded me of something, but I couldn't put my finger on it for a few days. But then I remembered: a conversation years ago with a friend who had spent a long time struggling with alcoholism and drug addiction. He told me that he was desperately unhappy all through his addictions and was well aware of that fact. I asked him a simple question: "If you were miserable, why did you keep doing it?" Like the financier above, he paused before answering. "I cared more about being high than being happy," he told me.

That's when it struck me: people who choose being special over happy are *addicts*. Maybe that sounds strange to you. Picture a person desperately hooked on booze. Probably the person you envision is down and out, self-medicating against the traumas of a harsh world. You probably don't envision someone who is successful and hardworking. They are less likely to fall prey to addictions, right?

Wrong. According to the Organisation for Economic Cooperation and Development (OECD), the likelihood of drinking *rises* with education level and socioeconomic status.[1] Some believe—and I agree, based on my work—that people in high-pressure jobs tend to self-medicate with alcohol, including drinking at hazardous levels, which can turn off the sensation of anxiety like a switch—temporarily.

But alcohol isn't the only addiction to which strivers are prone, or arguably even the worst. One of the nastiest and most virulent addictions I have seen is *workaholism*. This term was coined by the psychologist Wayne Oates in the 1960s after his own son asked for an appointment at Oates's office to see him, so scarce was his father's time. Oates defined workaholism in 1971 as "the compulsion or the uncontrollable need to work incessantly."[2]

This syndrome is endemic to professionally successful people. Consider the sheer number of hours spent at work: according to the *Harvard Business Review*, the average American CEO works 62.5 hours per week, versus 44 hours by the average worker.[3] That rings true to me: I doubt I ever worked less than a sixty-hour week in the entire decade that I was a chief executive. Many leaders work much more than this, leaving little time to cultivate outside relationships.

Leaders who work crushing hours often tell me they have no choice if they want to do their jobs adequately well. But I don't buy it. When I dig a little—in my life and the lives of others—I usually find that workaholics are caught in a vicious cycle: They become successful by working more than others—and thus more than "necessary"—but believe they have to keep up that pace to maintain their astronomical productivity. The rewards of that productivity give way to a fear of falling behind as an impetus to keep running. Soon enough, the work crowds out relationships and outside activities. With little else, work is all that is left to the workaholic, reinforcing the cycle.

Workaholism feeds fear and loneliness; fear and loneliness feed workaholism.

Therapists generally diagnose workaholism with three questions:

1. Do you usually spend your discretionary time in work activities?
2. Do you usually think about work when not working?
3. Do you work well beyond what is required of you?[4]

I don't think this diagnostic framework gets at the root of the problem, though. I bet most readers of this book would answer these questions in the affirmative, whether they are "workaholics" or not, because they truly enjoy their work and are committed to excellence—which requires more than the bare minimum effort to not get fired. Working hard and enjoying it doesn't make you a workaholic.

However, I have met a lot of people who cross over into workaholism, and I am guilty of this myself. Here are, in my opinion, better questions:

1. Do you fail to reserve part of your energy for your loved ones after work and stop working only when you are a desiccated husk of a human being?
2. Do you sneak around to work? For example, when your spouse leaves the house on a Sunday, do you immediately turn to work and then put it away before she or he returns so that it is not apparent what you were doing?

3. Does it make you anxious and unhappy when someone—such as your spouse—suggests you take time away from work for activities with loved ones, even when nothing in your work is unusually pressing? (By the way, I'm feeling a bit angry and defensive as I write this.)

If this sounds an awful lot to you like alcoholism, it should. Psychotherapist Bryan E. Robinson has written extensively on the subject of workaholism and family relationships and shows that workaholics have many of the same patterns of behavior and estrangement with their spouses as alcoholics do.[5] The addict feels misunderstood and under attack and engages in secretive behavior. Meanwhile, the spouse feels neglected and hurt. Marital dissolution often occurs.[6] The workaholic then rationalizes the breakup as a case of ingratitude. As one man told me when I was writing this book, "My wife wants the nice things that come from money but is angry with me for doing what it takes to earn that money." Uh-huh.

Workaholics convince themselves that that fourteenth hour of work is vital to their success, when, in reality, their productivity is likely severely diminished by that point. Economists consistently find that our marginal productivity tanks with work hours beyond eight or ten per day.[7] If you are a twelve- to fourteen-hour-workday person, you have probably noticed that almost anything can divert your attention late in the afternoon and evening. Human focus—especially on sedentary tasks—simply can't be sustained for so long.

What all addictions have in common is that they involve an

unhealthy relationship with something unworthy of human love, be it booze, gambling, applause, or—yes—work. Work is the dominant relationship in a workaholic's life. Thus, they travel for business on anniversaries; they miss Little League games. Some forgo marriage for their careers—earning the description of being "married to their work"—knowing full well that a good marriage (to another human) is more satisfying than any job. This is baffling to people with normal work patterns. But getting between a workaholic and her work is like getting between a grizzly bear and her cubs.

Workaholism keeps you chained to your job. But even more, it keeps you stuck in all your old work patterns, because you fear doing anything that separates you from the day in, day out of your most important relationship. And that makes jumping to a new curve all but impossible.

Success addiction

Before we look for solutions, we need to dig a little deeper still. Alcoholics are addicted to alcohol, it's true. But in reality, they are hooked on what alcohol does to their brains.

And so it is with workaholism. What workaholics truly crave isn't work per se; it is success. They kill themselves working for money, power, and prestige because these are forms of approval, applause, and compliments—which, like all addictive things, from cocaine to social media, stimulate the neurotransmitter dopamine.[8]

Why? For some I have met, the thrill of success, albeit momentary, blots out the blackness of "normal" life—achievement is a way to pull oneself above a grim baseline mood. Something is clearly wrong when the idea of being "normal" induces enough panic to make someone neglect the people they love in favor of the possible admiration of strangers.

But it is strikingly common among some of history's greatest strivers. Take Winston Churchill, perhaps the most impactful statesman of the twentieth century. He often referred to his "black dog," a melancholy that he treated with whiskey, obsessive work, and an unquenchable thirst for greatness. Unable to leave his tortured mind unattended during his crushing schedule as a wartime prime minister, he simultaneously wrote forty-three books.

Similarly, Abraham Lincoln was desperately sad off and on throughout his life, and at times suicidal, admitting once to a friend that he never dared to carry a knife in his pocket for fear he would use it on himself.[9] Most historians believe he was the author of an anonymous poem titled "The Suicide's Soliloquy," published in 1838 in Lincoln's local newspaper in Springfield, Illinois, the *Sangamo Journal*. Here is a short taste of that poem:

> *Sweet steel! come forth from your sheath,*
> *And glist'ning, speak your powers;*
> *Rip up the organs of my breath,*
> *And draw my blood in showers!*

This came during a flurry of activity for Lincoln, who clearly had what psychiatrist John Gartner calls the "hypomanic edge," the near-manic energy that often punctuates depressive episodes among high achievers.[10] In the years before depression treatments, he tried everything, from cocaine to opium. But his go-to remedy was always work and worldly success.

There is a wonderful little passage in the *Confessions* of Saint Augustine, written around the year 400. He starts by describing his insatiable cravings for success in the eyes of others: "I panted after honors . . . boiling with the feverishness of consuming thoughts." (Every success addict can relate to this.) He then describes coming across a beggar in the streets of Milan, whom he secretly *admired*: "He was joyous, I anxious; he void of care, I full of fears."

Perhaps we are evolved for the success addiction. It makes sense, if success enhances our genetic fitness, making us more attractive to others (that is, until we ruin our marriages). But to be constantly noticed, to achieve specialness, doesn't come cheap. Apart from a few reality TV stars and accidental celebrities, success is brutal work and takes sacrifices. In the 1980s, physician Robert Goldman famously found in his research that half of aspiring athletes would be willing to accept certain death in five years in exchange for an Olympic gold medal today.[11] "Fame is the spur that the clear spirit doth raise," said John Milton in his poem *Lycidas*, ". . . to scorn delights and live laborious days."

But the goal can't be satisfied; the success addict is never "successful enough." The high only lasts a day or two, and then it's on to the next success hit. "Unhappy is he who depends on success to be happy," wrote Alex Dias Ribeiro, a former famous Formula 1 race car driver. "For such a person, the end of a successful career is the end of the line. His destiny is to die of bitterness or to search for more success in other careers and to go on living from success to success until he falls dead. In this case, there will not be life after success."[12]

Making yourself an object

From my earliest days, I learned of the evils of objectifying others. My father went to great pains to impress on me that as a man growing up, I was never to consider others—especially women—primarily in terms of their physical characteristics. To do so is to dehumanize them, which we believed was a grave sin.

There is nothing new or even especially religious about this moral teaching. It was, for example, one of the key themes of the philosopher Immanuel Kant, who wrote, "As soon as a person becomes an Object of appetite for another, all motives of moral relationship cease to function, because as an Object of appetite for another a person becomes a thing and can be treated and used as such by every one."[13]

This focuses almost entirely on sexual objectification and how it degrades well-being, but objectification takes other forms such as in work. That is the focus of Karl Marx, who wrote in 1844, "The spontaneous activity of the human imagination, of the human brain and the human heart, operates on the individual independently of him. . . . It belongs to another; it is the loss of his self."[14] This was his indictment of capitalism as an economic and social system that makes people unhappy by making them into part of a human machine in which humanity is expunged and only productivity remains. They are objectified, reduced.

I do not agree with his assessment of capitalism as a system (and have written books about this in the past), but I believe he was spot-on that objectification of people as workers ruins happiness. In 2021, two French researchers, publishing in the journal *Frontiers in Psychology*, developed a measure of objectification in the workplace based on the feeling of being used as a tool and not being recognized as an agent in the working environment.[15] As they note, workplace objectification leads to burnout, job dissatisfaction, depression, and sexual harassment.

The moral case against objectifying others is fairly straightforward. It starts to get more complicated when the objectifier and the one being objectified are the same person—in other words, with self-objectification, which scholars define as viewing oneself from a third-person perspective that does not consider one's full humanity.[16] Examples of this would be staring into the mirror and feeling inadequate or worthless—or, for that matter, fulfilled and happy—merely because of one's physical appearance. Or in the case of work, judging one's own self-worth—for good or ill—based on job performance or professional standing.

Self-objectification lowers self-worth and life satisfaction. In the case of physical self-objectification among women (where virtually all the research is focused), studies show that it leads to body shame and low self-esteem, which degrade life satisfaction.[17] Even in the case of people who are especially attractive, this kind of focus is inherently dehumanizing and self-critical:

there's *always* something wrong with your body. Naturally, all of this is made worse by social media, which makes self-objectification easier than ever.[18]

Studies among young women show that self-objectification leads to a sense of invisibility and lack of autonomy and has a direct relationship with eating disorders and depression.[19] It also lowers competence in normal, everyday tasks. One 2006 experiment on seventy-nine women aged nineteen to twenty-eight randomly assigned them to try on a sweater or a swimsuit, look in a full-length mirror, complete a questionnaire about self-image, and then perform a routine task identifying colors.[20] They found that the women in the swimsuits—who were induced to feel "I am my body"—identified the colors significantly more slowly than the women in the sweaters.

There have been no studies of happiness and competence when we professionally self-objectify, when we think "I am my job." But common sense tells us that this is a tyranny every bit as nasty as physical self-objectification. We become Marx's heartless work overlord to ourselves, cracking the whip mercilessly, seeing ourselves as nothing more than *Homo economicus*. Love and fun are sacrificed for another day of work, in search of a positive internal answer to the question "Am I successful yet?" We become cardboard cutouts of real people. And then, when the end inevitably comes—when professional decline sets in—we are left bereft and withered to ourselves and, inevitably, forgotten by others.

In his 1964 book, *Understanding Media*, Marshall McLuhan famously said that "the medium is the message."[21] He noted that in the famous Greek myth, Narcissus did not fall in love with himself, but with the image of himself. And so it is when we professionally self-objectify: Our work is our medium, which is our message. We love the image of ourselves as successful, not ourselves in true life. But you are not your job, and I (as I have to remind myself) am not mine.

Pride, fear, social comparison, and withdrawal

At its root, self-objectification is a problem of pride. Pride is often thought of as a good thing in our modern society; we use it to denote admiration. I tell my kids I am proud of them, for example. Or I might say without embarrassment that I am proud of this book. But this connotation is relatively new. In almost all philosophical traditions, pride is a deadly vice that rots a person from the inside out. Buddhists use the word *māna*, which in Sanskrit refers to an inflated mind that disregards others in favor of the self and leads to one's own suffering. Thomas Aquinas defined it as an excessive desire for one's own excellence, leading to misery.[22] In Dante's *Divine Comedy*, Satan is depicted as a victim of his terrible pride by being frozen from the waist down—fixed and in agony—in ice created by wind from the flapping of his grotesque, batlike wings.

Pride is sneaky: it hides inside good things. Saint Augustine astutely observed that "every other kind of sin has to do with the commission of evil deeds, whereas pride lurks even in good works in order to destroy them."[23] So true—work, which is a source of meaning and purpose, becomes workaholism, which hurts our relationships. Success, the fruit of excellence, becomes an addiction. All because of pride.

A cousin of pride is fear. A lot of people addicted to drugs and alcohol say they stay addicted because they are afraid of "normal" life, with its struggles, stresses, and boredom. Success addicts frequently have a lot of fear, too—fear of failure.

Fear of failure has been studied quite a bit. For example, researchers have found that public speaking is college students' most common fear; some scholars have famously asserted that people fear it even more than death.[24] I find it most among my students who are the greatest strivers because they are terrified of failing in anything, even a silly class presentation. And dread about failing doesn't just afflict the young or inexperienced: according to a 2018 survey, 90 percent of CEOs "admit fear of failure keeps them up at night more than any other concern."[25]

Fear animates all success addicts. As philosopher Jean-Jacques Rousseau wrote in his *Confessions*, "I was not afraid of punishment, I was only afraid of disgrace; and that I feared more than death, more than crime, more than anything else in the world."[26] Can you relate to this?

It is a sad irony that people who strongly fear failure don't take much pleasure from their actual accomplishments and have high anxiety about not performing well at a crucial moment.[27] In other words, they're motivated less by the possibility of winning and gaining something of value and more by their fear about the possibility of messing up.

Those are some of the same personality traits that drive perfectionism. In fact, perfectionism and the fear of failure go hand in hand: they lead you to believe that success isn't about doing something good but about *not* doing something bad. If you suffer from a fear of failure, you'll know exactly what I mean. Where striving for success should be an exciting journey toward an amazing destination—as the famous climber George Mallory said, to ascend a mountain "because it's there"—it feels instead like an exhausting slog, with all your energy focused on not tumbling over a cliff.

Meanwhile, perfectionists view themselves as different—research shows they believe they have higher ability, higher standards, and are capable of greater accomplishments than others. This is often true! And this favorable comparison with others gives them a momentary fix, but the idea of falling behind creates a sense of panic, like facing the prospect of catastrophic failure. When I consider myself better than others—when "better" is at the core of my identity—then failure is unthinkable. It would excommunicate myself from my objectified self. It is like a little death.

Many success addicts confess that they feel like losers when they see someone else who is yet more successful. Success is fundamentally *positional*, meaning it enhances our position in social hierarchies. Social scientists for decades have shown that positional goods do not bring happiness. Even money, which people swear they like simply for what it will buy, becomes largely positional beyond a relatively low level. As the Dalai Lama once reminded me, people have ten fingers but buy twenty rings. This positionality is part of how we are naturally wired.

The drive to achieve worldly success for positional reasons can easily become an obsessive passion. The problem is that this kind of success—like all addictive things—is ultimately Sisyphean and unsatisfying. No one is ever famous enough, rich enough, or powerful enough. "Wealth is like sea-water; the more we drink, the thirstier we become, and the same is true of fame"—that's philosopher Arthur Schopenhauer, writing in 1851, more than a century and half before social media was invented and made the whole problem ten times worse.[28]

Meanwhile, staying high in the success hierarchy is grinding work. A musician of some renown once told me that getting and staying famous is a miserable combination of boredom and terror. Emily Dickinson captured this drudgery in her poem "I'm Nobody! Who are you?":

How dreary — to be — Somebody!
How public — like a Frog —
To tell one's name — the livelong June —
To an admiring Bog!

It is often believed that President Teddy Roosevelt called social comparison the "thief of joy." Whether he said it or not, it's true: researchers have long found that social comparison lowers our happiness.[29] But you hardly need a study to tell you that—just spend a few hours browsing Instagram and see how bad you feel about yourself. This is because you are comparing your success with your perception of others' success, as depicted in information of dubious accuracy. Nothing good comes of this.

Social comparison, fear of failure, and perfectionism are like Dante's prideful sea of ice, freezing you in place with thoughts of what others will think of you—or, worse, what you will think of yourself—if you do not succeed at something. These are the fruits of success addiction. And to top it off, it leads to withdrawal.

For alcohol addiction, withdrawal can be an agonizing physical experience, to be sure. But talk to the former alcoholic and you will see it's so much deeper than that. Remember, booze is a relationship—probably the alcoholic's closest friendship. To quit is to lose that intimacy. The prospect of quitting is like looking into an abyss of emptiness—of never feeling really good ever again.

Success addicts experience withdrawal as well. I saw it all the time in my years running a Washington, DC–based think tank. People would step back from the political limelight—sometimes of their own volition, sometimes not—and suffer mightily. They talked of virtually nothing but the old days. They resented the people who came after them but who never asked for their help and advice.

Getting started on your recovery

Maybe you have never fully realized your addiction before reading this chapter and still aren't sure. Let's take a little quiz.

1. Do you define your self-worth in terms of your job title or professional position?
2. Do you quantify your own success in terms of money, power, or prestige?

3. Do you fail to see clearly—or are you uncomfortable with—what comes after your last professional successes?

4. Is your "retirement plan" to go on and on without stopping?

5. Do you dream about being remembered for your professional successes?

If you answered affirmatively to one of these questions, you are probably a success addict. By the way, when I started this project, I would have scored a perfect five, so don't feel too bad.

As successful as you are in your life and work, you are simply not going to move from old strengths to new strengths until you sort this out. It's not easy, but fortunately, it doesn't require a stint at the Betty Ford Center, either. Indeed, you don't need to swear off work (which is lucky, assuming that, like me, you need to make a living).

It does require an open admission of the truth, however, and a commitment to change: that what you have is a problem and you want to solve it, that what you have been doing isn't working, and that you want to be happy. This is *always* the first step in recovery from an addiction, by the way. The first step in Alcoholics Anonymous's program is "We admitted we were powerless over alcohol—that our lives had become unmanageable."

If you want to be happy, you have to state your honest aspiration to be happy, to be willing to be a little less special in worldly terms, and thus to stop objectifying yourself. You must state your *desire* to lighten your load with pride's opposing virtue: humility.

I have a little practice I have developed that helps me in this a great deal. An early twentieth-century Spanish Catholic cardinal, Rafael Merry del Val y Zulueta, composed a beautiful prayer called the "Litany of Humility." The prayer does not ask that we be spared humiliation, but that we be given the courage to deal with our fear of it. "From the fear of being humiliated, deliver me, Master," he implores. Inspired by this, I have a little litany I wrote that I use when I find myself becoming chained to workaholism, pride, fear of failure, perfectionism, or social comparison—the forces that keep me off my second curve. You can use it whether you are religious or not—the point is to name your addictions and state your desire to be free.

> *From putting my career before the people in my life, deliver me.*
> *From distracting myself from life with work, deliver me.*
> *From my drive to be superior to others, deliver me.*
> *From the allure of the world's empty promises, deliver me.*
> *From my feelings of professional superiority, deliver me.*
> *From allowing my pride to supplant my love, deliver me.*
> *From the pains of withdrawing from my addiction, deliver me.*
> *From the dread of falling into decline and being forgotten,*
> *   deliver me.*

The next step

Like most strivers, you likely spent decades trying to be successful in worldly terms, and now I am telling you to go against those instincts. But once you start on this journey, you will find that a lot of things in your life were there really only to build up your image—to yourself and others—to signify that you were successful and special. Some of these things are physical trophies, "positional goods" that show you are a big deal to the world. These can be houses and cars and boats, of course. But don't flatter yourself if these aren't important to you (they aren't to me), or if your success isn't the kind that gives you a lot of money. Your trophies might well be social media followers, or famous friends, or living in a cool place by the world's standards.

The point is that the symbols of your specialness have encrusted you like a ton of barnacles. Not only are these things incapable of bringing you any real satisfaction; they're making you too heavy to jump to your next curve.[30] You need to chip a bunch of them away. But which ones?

If you've ever moved from a big house to an apartment, you know that the hardest part is figuring out what you don't need. You pore over every object as it conjures up memories, and you think "I spent good money on this and might need it again!" Similarly, as you think about shedding the false image of your extremely special self, you will probably experience a fear of regret.

How to do it right is our next topic.

CHAPTER 4

Start
Chipping
Away

IF YOU EVER VISIT TAIWAN, the one attraction you must not miss is the National Palace Museum. Arguably the greatest collection of Chinese art and artifacts in the world, the museum's permanent collection contains more than seven thousand items that date from the Neolithic period eight thousand years ago all the way to the early twentieth century.

If there is one problem with the museum, it is precisely its abundance. No one can take in more than a fraction of it in a single visit. Without guidance, a tour quickly becomes a forced march past pots, prints, and carved pieces of stone. Everything winds up looking like everything else, and the most memorable part of the visit is the snack bar.

That's why, one afternoon several years ago, in order to enjoy the museum properly, I hired a guide to show me a few famous pieces and explain their artistic and philosophical significance. Little did I know, with one remark, my guide was about to give me advice that might just change my life.

Looking at a massive jade carving of the Buddha from the Qing dynasty, my guide offhandedly remarked that this was a good illustration of how the Eastern view of art differs from the Western view. "How so?" I asked.

Elliptically, he answered my question with a question: "What do you think of when I ask you to imagine a work of art yet to be started?"

"An empty canvas, I guess," I responded.

"Right. That's because you Westerners see art as being created from nothing. In the East, we believe the art already exists, and our job is simply to reveal it. It is not visible because we add something, but because we take away the parts that are not the art."

While my image of unstarted art was an empty canvas, my guide told me that his was an uncarved block of jade, like the one that ultimately became the Buddha in front of us. My work of art doesn't exist until I add images and paint. His already exists but is not visible until he takes away the stone that is not part of the sculpture within the block.

That metaphor is pretty straightforward in the case of sculpture. It is harder for, say, music. But it's not impossible. A musician from India once asked me how I could "hear the music" during a Brahms symphony. I asked what he meant; after all, with an eighty-five-piece orchestra cranking away at

100 decibels, it's pretty hard *not* to hear the music. He replied that the music, in his brain, was obscured by too many people playing at the same time. This is the essential difference between Western classical music, which adds sound until it is "right" (hence the huge orchestra in the case of the Brahms symphony), and an Indian classical raga, which discards all sounds that obscure the "true music" (hence an ensemble of just a few musicians).

Art mirrors life, as usual. In the West, success and happiness come—or so we believe—by avoiding losses and accumulating more stuff: more money, more accomplishments, more relationships, more experiences, more prestige, more followers, more possessions. Meanwhile, most Eastern philosophy warns that this acquisitiveness leads to materialism and vanity, which derails the search for happiness by obscuring one's essential nature.[1] We need to chip away the jade boulder of our lives until we find ourselves.

As we grow older in the West, we generally think we should have a lot to show for our lives—a lot of trophies. According to more Eastern thinking, this is backward. As we age, we shouldn't accumulate more to *represent* ourselves but rather strip things away to *find* our true selves—and thus, to find our second curve. In the words of Lao Tzu, author of the *Tao Te Ching*, written in the fourth century BC,

> *I shall overcome with the simplicity of original nature.*
> *With the simplicity of true nature, there shall be no desire.*
> *Without desire, one's original nature will be at peace.*
> *And the world will naturally be in accord with the right Way.*[2]

I was in the early stages of research for this book when I encountered this idea, and it completely captured my imagination. After all, I started my life fully immersed in the arts; not only was I a musician, but my mother was a professional painter. As such, I have always seen my life as a creative endeavor. This is the perfect metaphor for me. My happiest days are those that start out like an empty canvas, waiting to be filled up with ideas and creative interactions.

But as I spoke with my Taiwanese guide and thought later about the lessons he taught me, I realized that the Western metaphor might not be the right one as I live the back half of my life. It might actually be becoming a hindrance to my happiness and satisfaction.

In my fifties, my life is jammed with possessions, accomplishments, relationships, opinions, and commitments. I asked myself, "Can the right formula for a happy life really be to add more and more, until I die?" Obviously, the answer is no. Even worse than the inherent fruitlessness of this strategy, it gets less and less effective over time as our first success curve declines and the returns to our efforts diminish.

To get off the first curve and onto the second, instead of adding more and more to our lives, we need to understand why this doesn't work and then start taking things away.

The bucket list

The happiness strategy of getting and owning and doing more and more and more has a name: the "bucket list." If you google this term, the search will return about eighty million hits. As everyone knows, this is the list of all the stuff you want to see, do, and acquire before you die. This is precisely the same idea as adding brushstrokes to get a finished work of art: do all the stuff in your bucket to get a full and happy life.

I have known many people who follow this strategy, and no doubt so have you. I sometimes think of a man I met when I was still a teenager. He was a very early software entrepreneur, right on the cusp of the revolution that would change all of our lives. He had grown up poor and never amounted to much professionally, until his late thirties, when he was part of the team that had a big product breakthrough—a computer program still well-known today—that made him rich beyond his wildest dreams.

After that, his entire identity was "Successful Entrepreneur": a special person par excellence. But that required more than one big hit to stay special. He cast about, but no other significant professional successes came his way. So he turned to his bucket list. He bought houses. He bought cars by the dozens. He bought gadgets, art, and every expensive knickknack that struck his fancy. His purchasing outstripped his ability to even enjoy the things he bought: He used his dining room as a kind of warehouse for unopened boxes full of things he had acquired. Paintings sat on the floor, unhung. Cars were not driven.

He actually said to me once, quoting the entrepreneur Malcolm Forbes approvingly, "He who dies with the most toys, wins."[3] I remember thinking, "Actually, he who dies with the most toys, dies."

His use of time and relationships mirrored his buying behavior. He traveled constantly, checking off sites on his bucket list—castles in Germany, temples in Cambodia, icebergs in the Arctic. He took lots and lots of pictures to show people what he had seen. Similarly, he had hundreds of people in his life whom he counted as friends but barely knew, but with whom he had pictures. He collected people.

And yet he wasn't happy—on the contrary. He boasted endlessly about his big hit years before—the definition of his objectified self—and looked toward some new venture that might strengthen that self-image. Meanwhile, his growing collection of items, experiences, and people piled up as a substitute for the success he obviously craved. But that craving was never satisfied.

This isn't a new problem. Let's meet two men who solved it.

From princes to sages

Born to nobility in 1225, Thomas Aquinas was the son of Count Landulf of Aquino and grew up in the family's castle in the central Italian town of Roccasecca. Landulf's brother (Thomas's uncle) Sinibald was the abbot of the first Benedictine monastery, in Monte Cassino, a post of enormous social prestige. As the son of a noble family, Thomas was expected to enter the church and was slotted to succeed his uncle in that coveted post.

But Thomas had no interest in this worldly glory. At the age of nineteen, he announced his intention to join the recently created Dominican order, a mendicant group of monks dedicated to poverty and itinerant preaching. This, he felt, was his true identity. The life of wealth and privilege needed to be chipped away to find his true self.

His family was having none of it. An Aquino would not be an impoverished nobody! (Parents often objectify their kids, don't they?) At one point, they even kidnapped him from the Dominicans and imprisoned him in a castle, where he was held for a year. Unmoved from his resolve even while imprisoned, his brothers resorted to trying to shake his faith, hiring a prostitute at one point to seduce Thomas. He chased her out of the castle with a fireplace poker.

His family finally acquiesced, and he pursued the work of a cloistered scholar, producing dense works of philosophy, which made him very happy indeed.[4] Not only did he choose divine fulfillment over worldly specialness, he became an expert in this distinction. In his view, people who opt for the worldly path choose "substitutes for God": idols that objectify the idolater and never satisfy the craving for happiness.[5] Even if you are not a religious believer, his list rings true as the idols that attract us.

They are *money, power, pleasure,* and *honor.*

The last of these four, honor, is perhaps less obvious as an unhealthy attachment. In today's world, *honor* has a very positive connotation. I have a son in the U.S. Marine Corps who is expected "to serve with honor." That's not how Thomas meant it, however. Honor here refers to fame—to be known to many. But before you dismiss this as not a problem for you ("I don't care about being famous!"), it also refers to fame's insidious cousins: prestige and admiration—the favorable attention of people who "matter." For many readers who are successful but anxious, professional or social prestige is indeed a huge attachment.

Thomas argues that these idols leave us dissatisfied because they are not what we need as complete persons. They are the counterfeit currency paid to our special, objectified selves. As he puts it in the case of money,

> In the desire for wealth and for whatsoever temporal goods . . . when we already possess them, we despise them, and seek others. . . . The reason of this is that we realize more their insufficiency when we possess them: and this very fact shows that they are imperfect, and the sovereign good does not consist therein.[6]

In other words, it brings no satisfaction. He gives the same treatment to power, pleasure, and honor, concluding in each case that they are, in fact, inadequate for delivering what our hearts desire.

But Thomas didn't just pontificate about this—remember, he lived it. He attained true greatness only by forgoing the world's *definition* of greatness, by chipping away the world's rewards to find his essential self. If Thomas had become a fancy Benedictine abbot, the only record of his life would be on a list of abbots from the Middle Ages, and the only person who knew of him today would be approximately one PhD student working on an obscure doctoral dissertation.[7] Instead, he is known as the greatest philosopher of his age, who still casts a long shadow over Western thought and the Catholic Church.

Thomas's wisdom can be applied very practically to help us understand what *we* need to chip away to find happiness. I have a party game I like to call "What's My Idol?" Here's how it works: rank Thomas's four attachments with respect to how much control they have over you, starting at the bottom with what attracts you the least. Maybe you don't like having power over other people—that's number four. And perhaps while money is nice, you're not going to kill yourself for it—that's number three. Now keep going . . . pleasure is a trickier one for you perhaps. You can control it, even though it pulls at you— let's say that's number two. That leaves fame—or prestige or admiration . . . the monkey on your back of always wanting the favorable attention of others . . . the thing you are a little ashamed of but that always pulls at you and never satisfies. That's *your* idol, and the more of it you get the more of an object you become.

Thomas's story is not unique, or especially Western. Consider Siddhartha Gautama, a prince born in 624 BC to Suddhodana, the ruler of the Shakya clan, which lived in the region that is now on the border between Nepal and India. Siddhartha's mother having died just days after the prince's birth, Suddhodana vowed to protect his son from life's miseries and thus kept him shut inside a palace where all his worldly needs and desires would be met.

Siddhartha never ventured out of the palace until he was twenty-nine years old, when, overcome by curiosity, he asked a charioteer to show him the outside world. In the town outside the palace, he encountered an old man—the first example of aging he had ever seen. The charioteer explained that all people grow old. Returning to the palace, Siddhartha was disturbed by this revelation and asked to leave a second time.

On his second sojourn, he encountered a man wracked with disease, a decaying corpse, and a religious ascetic. He was once again distressed by the disease and death but perplexed by the ascetic. What did the man seek, if not the worldly pleasures the prince enjoyed in abundance? The charioteer's answer changed Siddhartha's life: the ascetic, through renunciation of worldly goods, sought to achieve release from the fear of disease and death that Siddhartha found so troubling.

Overcome by all this, Siddhartha left his kingdom the next day to learn for himself how to face life's suffering as an ascetic. He spent the next six years living a life of poverty, renouncing all pleasures, starving himself, and exposing himself to pain. But insight did not come. One day as he starved himself, a young girl offered him a bowl of rice. He accepted it, upon which he had a flash of insight that renunciation per se was not the key to finding release from life's torments. He ate, drank, and bathed and then sat under the Bodhi tree, vowing not to move until he found the truth.

Over the next several days, the truth emerged to Siddhartha—that release from suffering comes not from renunciation of the things of the world, but from release from *attachment* to those things. A Middle Way shunned both ascetic extremism and sensuous indulgence, because both are attachments and thus lead to dissatisfaction. At the moment of this realization, Siddhartha became the Buddha.

The Buddha devised a practical guide—the Four Noble Truths—for dealing with these troublesome attachments.

Noble Truth 1. Life is suffering (*dukkha* in Sanskrit), due to chronic dissatisfaction.

Noble Truth 2. The cause of this suffering is craving, desire, and attachment for worldly things.

Noble Truth 3. Suffering can be defeated by eliminating this craving, desire, and attachment.

Noble Truth 4. The way to eliminate craving, desire, and attachment is by following the *magga*, the Noble Eightfold Path of Buddhism.

Let's put these truths into the language of our problem: I have learned through my worldly success to search for satisfaction in the world's rewards, which are ultimately not satisfying. I will suffer with dissatisfaction when I attain these rewards if I am attached to them and suffer even more when I no longer earn them. The only solution to this problem is to shed my attachments and redefine my desires. To do so is my path to enlightenment—and my second curve.

Note that neither Thomas nor the Buddha argued that there is something inherently evil about worldly rewards. In fact, they can be used for great good. Money is critical for a functioning society and supporting your family; power can be wielded to lift others up; pleasure leavens life; and fame can attract attention to the sources of moral elevation. But as *attachments*—the focus of our life's attention and as ends instead of means—the problem is simple: they cannot bring us the deep *satisfaction* we desire.

We chase our worldly attachments up our first success curve. We work ourselves to death to attain the elusive satisfaction;

when the success curve starts to bend back down, the attachments give us tremendous suffering. These attachments must be chipped away to make it possible to jump onto the second curve.

The science of satisfaction

It only took a couple of millennia, but popular culture and modern social science finally caught up with the wisdom of Siddhartha and Thomas Aquinas, and they can help us understand the attachment problem even better.

If you know just one song by the Rolling Stones, it's probably their 1965 megahit "(I Can't Get No) Satisfaction." It's one of the most popular songs of all time, not because it's such a great piece of music, but because it states a truth about life. Somewhere deep in our lizard brains (to be more precise, in the limbic system), way below our level of consciousness, satisfaction is defined by this deviously simple equation:

Satisfaction = Getting what you want

It is so incredibly simple, even a baby follows it! Don't believe me? Give a one-year-old a french fry she's reaching for and watch her expression. That's more or less the same expression you got when you received your last huge raise or promotion at work. You really wanted it, you worked for it, and when you got it, the reward was deeply satisfying.

Deeply satisfying, that is, for a couple of days at most. And that's the real problem, isn't it? The song should really have been titled "(I Can't *Keep* No) Satisfaction." We know more or less how to meet our desire for satisfaction but are terrible at making it last. It's almost as if our brains won't let us enjoy anything for very long.

And that is exactly what's happening. To understand why, we need to introduce the concept of "homeostasis," which is the natural tendency for all living systems to maintain stable conditions in order to survive. The term was introduced in 1932 by a physician named Walter Cannon in his book *The Wisdom of the Body*, where he showed that we have built-in mechanisms to regulate temperature, water, salt, sugar, protein, fat, calcium, and oxygen levels.[8]

Homeostasis keeps us alive and healthy but also explains how drugs and alcohol work. When you have a stiff drink or a shot of heroin for the first time, it is a massive shock to your unprepared system, which is why addicts always pine for that first-time feeling. And not just hard drugs: I remember the first time I drank a lot of coffee. In seventh grade, a friend's parents got an espresso machine (this was 1977, so that was very rare). I grew up in Seattle, and we went down to Starbucks—the only Starbucks in the world back then—and got a pound of coffee and had eight shots of espresso each. I remember climbing up on his roof that night, cutting a gash in my stomach on his gutter, and, while bleeding profusely, thinking about how vivid and beautiful the stars were.

(For that matter, you can get a miniature version of that

experience the first time in a day you use any addictive sub-
stance. That's why Starbucks talks in its marketing about "that
first sip feeling.")

While that first sip—or bump, or hit—might give you pleasure, your brain senses an assault on its equilibrium and fights
back by neutralizing the entering drug, making it impossible
to get the first feeling back. I could drink coffee all day now,
and no way am I going up on the roof. Further, homeostasis is
also what gives you a rebound effect from any recreational sub-
stance, from a hangover after drinking, to withdrawal from
heroin, to fatigue after caffeine wears off.

Addiction is basically a maladaptation of homeostasis, in
which the brain becomes very adept at dealing with constant
onslaughts to its equilibrium. Whereas the first drink of alcohol at age fourteen gave you a huge, awesome buzz, the first
drink of the day after years of abuse gives you a tiny bump, and
when it wears off you feel terrible. Meanwhile, your brain is
suffering from "anti-alcohol," so you need alcohol simply to
feel "normal."

The same set of principles works on our emotions. When
you get an emotional shock—good or bad—your brain wants to
re-equilibrate, making it hard to stay on the high or low for
very long. This is especially true for positive emotions, which
makes evolutionary sense for survival. The joy that came to
your caveman ancestor from finding a sweet berry on a bush
couldn't occupy him for very long, lest he be distracted from the
threat of the tiger, for whom your ancestor would make a nice
lunch.

That's why, when it comes to success, you can't ever get

enough. If you base your sense of self-worth on success, you tend to go from victory to victory to avoid feeling awful. That is pure homeostasis at work. The buzz from success is neutralized quickly, leaving a hangover feeling. Knowing you will be looking for the bump again very soon, your brain ultimately adjusts to a baseline feeling of anti-success. After a while, you need constant success hits just not to feel like a failure. That's what we social scientists refer to as the "hedonic treadmill." You run and run but make no real progress toward your goal—you simply avoid being thrown off the back from stopping or slowing down.

So let's return to our equation and update it to reflect all this more accurately:

Satisfaction = Continually getting what you want

The carrot dangled in front of you is the fleeting feeling that you've made it, despite the fact that you are emotionally running in place on the hedonic treadmill. And it is that much worse when your abilities are starting to decline—the carrot is gradually getting further away, despite the fact that you are running faster than ever. Thus, the dissatisfaction problem compounds the decline problem.

I saw a cartoon some years ago of a man on his deathbed, telling his grieving loved ones, "I wish I'd bought more crap." Successful people often keep working to increase their wealth, accumulating far beyond anything they could possibly spend and more than they want to bequeath. One day I asked a wealthy friend why this is so. His answer was that many people who have gotten rich know how to measure their self-worth only in material terms, so they stay on the hedonic treadmill of earning and acquiring, year after year. They hope that at some point, they will finally feel truly successful, happy, and thus ready to die.

But it never works.

Glitches in the evolutionary matrix

According to evolutionary psychology, our tendency to strive for more, more, more is perfectly understandable. For most of history, the majority of humans were at the edge of starvation. A "rich" caveman had a few extra animal skins and arrowheads, and maybe a few baskets of corn and dried fish to spare. This definition of "more" would most definitely give him a survival advantage, because he would better make it through a bad winter.

Our caveman ancestor didn't just want to make it through the winter, though; he had bigger ambitions than that. He wanted to find a mate and have kids, too. And what would make that possible? Not just having enough—no, he had to have more than the guy in the next cave over, which would make him a better prospect in the mating market.

This explains our weird fixation all throughout life on social comparison based on position and wealth. When we are talking about satisfaction from a success, there's another element to consider: success is all relative. After all, social hierarchy is based on the people in your community, whatever that means—geographical, professional, or virtual. I know people with hundreds of millions of dollars who feel like failures because their friends are billionaires. There are famous Hollywood celebrities who are depressed because someone else is *more* famous.

We all know perfectly well that social comparison is ridiculous and harmful—we touched on it in the last chapter—and research backs this up. Scholars show that participating in "keeping up with the Joneses" creates anxiety and even depression.[9] In experiments using human subjects solving puzzles, the unhappiest people were consistently those paying the most attention to how they performed relative to other subjects.[10] The small rush of pleasure we get from being envied by others one minute is swallowed up by the unhappiness from having less than someone else the next minute. But the urge to have more than others tugs at us relentlessly.

Unfortunately, it often feels like we can't stop the comparison game. From this, we get another equation:

Success = Continually having more than others

In other words, satisfaction from success requires not just that you continually run in place on the hedonic treadmill, but that you run slightly faster than other people are running on theirs.

But it gets worse. On your treadmill, you're not just pursuing something in a grand exercise in futility. Something is pursuing you, too: failure. You may know perfectly well that you are not actually moving forward on your treadmill. But if you stop running, you know that you'll go flying off the back like in some terrible, hilarious social media meme. That looks increasingly likely, because the inevitable decline in abilities means that even when you run faster, you gradually fall behind.

That, of course, provokes fear, and thus:

Failure = Having less

Even more powerful than our urge for *more* is our resistance to *less*. We try even harder to avoid losses than we do to achieve gains. That's the insight that earned the Nobel Prize in Economics for Princeton University's Daniel Kahneman, for work he did with Amos Tversky on *prospect theory*.[11] Prospect theory challenges the assumption that people are rational agents who assess gains and losses the same way; in fact, it asserts that people are much more affected emotionally by losing something than they are by gaining the same thing.

We have what Kahneman and Tversky call "loss aversion," which is why the news media freaks out when the stock market loses 10 percent, compared with when it rises by 10 percent. It's also why we hate disappointment so much and, as research shows, are willing to go to great lengths to avoid being disappointed.[12] My late father, for example, was a notorious pessimist. I remember once on a long road trip in rural Montana, he announced that we were probably going to run out of gas and have to spend the night in the car on the side of the road. I looked at the gas gauge and saw that the tank was more than half full. I asked why he always assumed the absolute worst-case scenario like that. "It's better to be pleasantly surprised than disappointed," he told me.

Once again, it makes perfect evolutionary sense. In a time when humans were always on the edge of starvation—most of human history for most of the world, before the industrial age began—a gain was nice, but a loss was potentially lethal. Someone sneaks into your cave and takes your winter stock of dried buffalo meat, and you starve. Prospect theory explains why you feel terrible if you lose your watch, even if you have four other watches. You are mistaking it in your mind for your caveman's stash of buffalo jerky.

Neurobiological instinct drives us, even as prosperity has spread and been democratized through industrialization, globalization, and enterprise. A bad winter is blessedly not a mortal threat to almost anyone in the industrialized world—or indeed most places in the world today—and that is getting truer by the year. Yet we still have the urge to acquire *more* to get good feelings and to signal our success to others, and to avoid *less* to avoid bad feelings like fear and shame.

It makes no sense in modern life to use our energies to have five cars, five bathrooms, or even five shirts, but we just . . . want them. Neuroscientists tell us why.[13] Dopamine—the neurotransmitter of pleasure behind nearly all addictive behaviors—is excreted in response to thoughts about buying new things, winning money, acquiring more power or notoriety, or, for that matter, having new sex partners.[14] The brain evolved to reward us for the behaviors that kept us alive and made it more likely to pass on our DNA. This may be an anachronism in modern life, but it is a fact of our lives nonetheless.

Here's the problem: The equations in this chapter govern our dopamine hits for short-term pleasure. But they don't bring any lasting satisfaction. This is especially true as we head into the back half of life. Early on, when one has relatively little and a lot to prove, more worldly rewards can be temporarily satisfying, but as one ages, we start to realize that the satisfaction never lasts, and the realization of futility sets in. Meanwhile, fear haunts us as we start to fall behind. Thus, psychologist Carl Jung noted, "what is a normal goal to a young person becomes a neurotic hindrance in old age."

My favorite illustration of this fact comes from Abd al-Rahman III, the emir and caliph of Córdoba in tenth-century Spain. Al-Rahman was an absolute ruler who lived in complete luxury. Here's how he assessed his own life at about age seventy:

> I have now reigned above 50 years in victory or peace; beloved by my subjects, dreaded by my enemies, and respected by my allies. Riches and honors, power and pleasure, have waited on my call, nor does any earthly blessing appear to have been wanting to my felicity.[15]

Fame, riches, and pleasure beyond imagination. Sounds great, doesn't it? But, as he goes on to write,

> I have diligently numbered the days of pure and genuine happiness which have fallen to my lot: They amount to 14.

Better math

To sum up, here are three formulas that explain both our impulses and the reason we can't ever seem to achieve lasting satisfaction.

Satisfaction = Continually getting
what you want
Success = Continually having more than others
Failure = Having less

Dissatisfaction is the malady that makes us chase our worldly rewards to ever-greater heights. The futility of attaining satisfaction is one of the reasons that professional decline is so painful: Desperate to achieve enough to be satisfied, we find that instead we are going backward. We are slowly falling off the back of the hedonic treadmill.

In our hearts, we know this, of course. But, *even with this knowledge*, the problem seems unsolvable. One astonishing proof of this is that the inventor of the term "hedonic treadmill," Philip Brickman—the celebrated psychologist also responsible for showing that winning the lottery brings no lasting satisfaction—died by suicide, throwing himself off a building across the street from his office at the University of Michigan.[16] Or consider the entrepreneur Tony Hsieh, founder of the online retailing pioneer Zappos and author of the mega bestseller *Delivering Happiness*. He died in 2020 at the age of forty-six after a long period of drug abuse and other self-destructive behavior resulting in at least one 911 call in which he threatened self-harm.[17]

But before you abandon all hope, I have good news: satisfaction is possible—just not with the old formulas. We need to toss out all that bad math and use this one equation instead, which incorporates the wisdom of Siddhartha and Thomas and the best modern social science:

Satisfaction = What you have ÷ what you want

Your satisfaction is what you *have*, divided by what you *want*. Notice the difference from the earlier equations? All of the evolutionary and biological formulas focus us on the numerator of our haves. If you are unsatisfied in life, that's what you most likely have been doing all these years. But that ignores the denominator of the equation—the wants. As you increase your haves without managing your wants, your wants will proliferate and sprawl. You can easily be less and less satisfied as you move up the success ladder, because your wants will *always* outstrip your haves. And when they do, your satisfaction will fall.

I have seen this a hundred times. Someone sees tremendous material success but feels less and less satisfied, the richer and more famous she gets. The Mercedes brings her less satisfaction at age fifty than the Chevy did at age thirty. Why? Because now she wants a Ferrari. She doesn't even know what's going on—she always just gets back on the treadmill and starts running, running, running.

The world is full of clever ways to make your wants explode

without your realizing it. Remember, when you keep running on the treadmill, people are making money because you are trying to satisfy ever-greater wants with more and more haves. No one is safe. Even arguably the world's most enlightened man, His Holiness the Dalai Lama, admits to it. "Sometimes I visit supermarkets," he says. "I really love to see supermarkets, because I can see so many beautiful things. So, when I look at all these different articles, I develop a feeling of desire, and my initial impulse might be, 'Oh, I want this; I want that.'"[18]

This isn't sinister. Corporations are not responsible for our satisfaction; *we* are. And that means not trying fruitlessly to get ahead on a speeding treadmill by falling over and over again for marketing gimmicks. It means turning the treadmill off by managing our wants. In the words of the Spanish Catholic saint Josemaría Escrivá, "He has most who needs least. Don't create needs for yourself."[19]

1. Ask why, not what

If you are ready to manage your wants—to start chipping away— the first step is to ask what exactly needs chipping. And that raises the question "What is my *why*?" The bestselling author and speaker Simon Sinek always gives people in search of true success in work and life the advice that they need to find their why.[20] That is, he tells them that to unlock their true potential and happiness, they need to articulate their deep purpose in life and shed the activities that are not in service of that purpose. Your why is the sculpture inside the block of jade.

Most people spend their time on the *what* of their lives—they can't see beyond the brushstrokes they've put on the canvas. For example, I often see myself as "college professor" or "guy who writes books" or something like that. Others can focus only on the whats of their daily lives. Consider this email I received from a successful fifty-year-old journalist.

> My best friend and I often ask each other, "Aren't we going to regret we didn't enjoy this time in our life more?" We agree that we will, and then we hang up the phone and go back to the madness. I don't think anyone wants madness but we want nice houses and schools and vacations and organic food and college and church and sleepaway camp and then you become tied to your circumstances.

Consider what she is saying: She *knows* that happiness comes from seeing past these distractions. But it's too complicated, too disruptive of ordinary life, so she never sets about making the changes she needs to make to achieve the happiness she knows she wants.

The same day I got that email, I received another, from a person in very similar life circumstances: a fifty-something-year-old woman, professionally very successful, who struggled with attachments. But then she got a wake-up call from her dead father.

> I [no longer] feel the need to surround myself with stuff . . . especially after my father died in his house, and

the paramedics almost couldn't reach him because his house was so full of stuff. That was a great lesson to learn.

Her father was unreachable in death because of his physical clutter. My correspondent asked herself whether she was unreachable due to the psychological clutter of a life spent building up a huge boulder, leading her to start chipping away the whats, to find the why.

I have heard this story over and over: people don't realize their unhealthy attachments in life until they suffer a loss or illness that makes the important things come into focus. Researchers have consistently found that most survivors of illness and loss experience *post-traumatic growth.* Indeed, cancer survivors tend to report higher happiness levels than demographically matched people who did not have cancer.[21] Talk to them, and they will tell you that they no longer bother with the stupid attachments that used to weigh them down, whether possessions, or worries about money, or unproductive relationships. The threat of losing their lives prematurely took a jackhammer to the jade encasing their true selves—the why of their lives.

But you don't need a tragic loss or health scare to start this process. Recently I met Luther Kitahata, a fifty-five-year-old entrepreneur from California. Luther isn't world-famous, but he has lived the American dream: his parents are immigrants who pushed him to learn a lot, work hard, and succeed. Which he did: he became a computer scientist and started seven companies. All through his career, he ran hard on the treadmill of success, pursuing the extrinsic rewards—and got them, only to be immediately unsatisfied and start running again.

Finally, around age fifty, feeling frustrated and empty, Luther started chipping away at his wants. "My brain hadn't been wired to be motivated by passion, meaning, and purpose," he told me. "My brain had been previously wired to be motivated by fear." It took a few years, but Luther ultimately walked away from his old career and now coaches others on how to rebuild—perhaps "de-build"—their lives. He also spends more time with his family and developing his spiritual life. There's less money, power, and fame, to be sure. However, he finds himself satisfied for the very first time.

Luther successfully jumped onto his second curve after he stopped adding and started chipping away. As he succinctly puts it, "I am loving my life."

You can say this, too, but you need to start chipping away—managing your worldly wants—before more time passes. Remember, the longer you leave it, the further down your fluid intelligence curve will drag you, and the harder the jump will be.

2. The reverse bucket list

A second way to get started on the task of chipping away is to look at the counsel we get that is making us into dissatisfied *Homo economicus*, and simply doing the opposite. For example, self-help gurus often give the advice to make an inventory of the bucket list on your birthday, so as to reinforce your worldly aspirations. Making a list of the things you want is temporarily satisfying, because it stimulates dopamine, the neurotransmitter of desire, which is pleasurable.

But it creates attachments, which create dissatisfaction as they grow. Remember my friend I told you about earlier, who fruitlessly sought satisfaction by checking off all his items. As the Buddha says in the Dhammapada, "The craving of one given to heedless living grows like a creeper. . . . Whoever is overcome by this wretched and sticky craving, his sorrows grow like grass after the rains."[22] Personally, I have gone in the other direction instead by compiling a "reverse bucket list" to make the ideas in this chapter practical and workable in my life.

Each year on my birthday, I list my worldly wants and attachments—the stuff that fits under Thomas's categories of *money, power, pleasure*, and *honor*. I try to be completely honest. I don't list stuff I don't actually want, like a boat or a house on Cape Cod. Rather, I go to my weaknesses, which usually involve the admiration of others. I'm embarrassed to admit that, but it's true.

I imagine myself in five years. I am happy and at peace. I am enjoying my life for the most part; I'm satisfied and living a life of purpose and meaning. I imagine myself saying to my wife, "You know, I have to say that I am truly happy at this point in my life." I then think of the forces in this future life that are most responsible for this happiness: my faith; my family; my friendships; the work I am doing that is inherently satisfying, meaningful, and that serves others.

Next, I go back to my bucket list. I consider how these things compete with the forces of my happiness for time, attention, and resources. I ponder how empty they are by comparison. I imagine myself sacrificing my relationships to choose the admiration of strangers and the result down the line in my life. With this in mind, I confront the bucket list. About each item, I say, "This is not evil, but it will not bring me the happiness and peace I seek, and I simply don't have time to make it my goal. I choose to detach myself from this desire."

Finally, I go back to the list of things that will bring me real happiness. I commit to pursuing these things with my time, affection, and energy.

This exercise has made a big difference in my life. It might help you, too.

3. Get smaller

A third method that helps break the habit of adding brushstrokes to an already full canvas is to start focusing on smaller things in life. Voltaire's 1759 satirical novel, *Candide*, recounts the tale of the young and naïve hero in his adventures with his tutor, the indefatigable optimist Professor Pangloss.[23] The story is one of horror after horror: war, rape, cannibalism, slavery. At one point, Pangloss even has one of his buttocks amputated. In the end, they retire to a small farm, where they find that the secret to happiness is not the world's glories, but rather to focus on the little contentments; to "cultivate our garden."

Satisfaction comes not from chasing bigger and bigger things, but paying attention to smaller and smaller things. Buddhist master Thich Nhat Hanh explains this in his book *The Miracle of Mindfulness*: "While washing the dishes, one should only be washing the dishes, which means that while washing the dishes one should be completely aware of the fact that one is washing the dishes."[24] Why? If we are thinking about the past or future, "we are not alive during the time we are washing the dishes." We are either reliving a past that is dead or "sucked away into the future" that exists merely in concept. Only to be mindful, therefore, is to be truly alive.

Once, my wife and I were at the home of close friends, eating and drinking out in their garden. It was dusk, and they asked us to gather around a plant with small, closed flowers. "Watch a flower," one of them instructed. We did so, for about ten minutes, in complete silence. All at once, the flowers popped open, which we learned that they did every evening. We gasped in amazement and joy. It was a moment of intense satisfaction.

But here's the interesting thing: Unlike most of the junk on my old bucket list, that satisfaction endured. That memory still brings me joy—more so than many of my life's earthly "accomplishments"—not because it was the culmination of a large goal, but because it was a small and serendipitous thrill. It was a tiny miracle that felt like a free gift, freely given.

Looking ahead

I spent this chapter trashing the idea that the bucket list will bring you anything but dissatisfaction. Let me say one good thing about the conventional bucket list, however: it makes us focus on the limits of time and thus on how to use time well. The idea of the bucket list is to make sure you don't get to the end and say, "I'm not ready to die! I've never ridden in a hot-air balloon!" (I didn't just make up this example—that's number 6 on the average bucket list, according to a 2017 survey.)[25]

Death is the most normal, natural thing in life itself, and yet we are amazingly adroit at acting as if it were abnormal and a big surprise. When I tell my graduate students, who are mostly in their late twenties, to contemplate the fact that they have fifty or sixty Thanksgivings left, and twenty or thirty with their parents, they looked pretty shocked. And it's not just young people—remember that the average American considers the *beginning* of "old age" to be six years after the average person dies. We avoid thinking realistically about the length of our lives and our time left, lulling us into the false belief that we have all the time in the world. This expunges the urgency of life changes, such as jumping onto the second curve.

Planning for the end, then, is our next challenge—and opportunity.

CHAPTER 5

Ponder Your Death

A COUPLE OF YEARS AGO I was having lunch with an old friend, a CEO who is almost exactly my age. I was telling him all about the research in this book—the inevitability of the decline of his fluid intelligence and how hard it is for a lot of successful people to cope with. "That won't be my problem," he said.

"Why not?" I asked.

"I won't decline," he responded. "I'll just go harder and harder, until the wheels come off."

In other words: work, work, work, *croak*. No second curve, because there's no need for one.

I call this the "Rage Against the Dying of the Light" strategy to deal with decline in fluid intelligence, named for Dylan

Thomas's well-known 1951 poem "Do Not Go Gentle into That Good Night," which famously enjoins the reader, "Rage, rage against the dying of the light." Thomas was talking literally about death—he wrote the poem for his dying father. And indeed, people have been raging against death forever.

I know what you're thinking: "I'm not afraid of dying!" Maybe, maybe not. Many psychologists would say you are deluding yourself if you say you aren't.

But no matter, that's not my point. Rather, it's this: Have you ever said, "My work is my life"? If you have, then your fear of decline is actually a *type* of fear of death. If you live to work—if your work is your life, or at least the source of your identity—proof of being fully alive is your professional ability and achievement. So when it declines, you are in the process of dying.

As a striver, it was your force of will and indefatigable work ethic that got you to the top of your fluid intelligence curve—and profession—in the first place. Raging is what you know best. But it fails at work, just as it does in life. Ability based on fluid intelligence increases, and then declines, in every profession. Some earlier, and some later; there are some key differences, but it is a misconception that decline can be delayed indefinitely in a profession just because it doesn't require physical strength. We saw that "idea professions" see decline, too—generally, decades before any dementia or senility.

Only when you face the truth of your professional decline—a kind of death—can you get on with your progress to the second curve. If you don't, you will be like my friend, trying to fight the inevitable, or at least *hoping* that there is some way around it.

And to face this truth means defeating the fear of your own demise—literal and professional. This fear handcuffs you to your fluid intelligence curve. If you can master it, the reward is incalculable: it will set you free.

But the only way to do it is by facing it head-on.

Understanding the fear of demise

"The idea of death, the fear of it, haunts the human animal like nothing else," anthropologist Ernest Becker wrote in his classic 1973 book, *The Denial of Death*.[1] A majority of people fear death to some extent, and most surveys find that about 20 percent have a high level of fear.[2] Some people have a fear that is so extreme as to rise to the level of a psychiatric condition known as "thanatophobia."

Whether paralyzing or mild, the fear of death has eight distinct dimensions: fear of being destroyed, fear of the dying process, fear of the dead, fear for significant others, fear of the unknown, fear of conscious death, fear for body after death, and fear of premature death.[3]

The first of these is uniquely human—it is the fear of nonexistence; the fear of being completely erased; the fear of being forgotten. My dog can feel fear when he's threatened, but as far as I know, he doesn't understand the concept of not existing, because he doesn't know he "exists" in the first place. Existential fear is not the stuff of biologists, then, but of philosophers. While death is inevitable, it also seems impossible insofar as we cannot conceive of not existing. This creates an unresolvable, unbearable cognitive dissonance. Cambridge University philosopher Stephen Cave calls this the "mortality paradox."[4]

The fear of decline involves this same fear of nonexistence. If my existence in relation to others is defined by my professional accomplishment or standing, my decline will effectively erase me. Not surprisingly, the ways people deal with the crisis of nonexistence are the same as how they deal with professional decline.

Consider the case of Walt Disney, whose fear of death and decline was legendary. One day in 1909, the seven-year-old Disney was playing by himself in the backyard of his family's Missouri farmhouse. He spied a big brown owl with its back to him. Like any red-blooded boy—certainly like my boys when they were seven—he snuck up on it with the intention of grabbing it, thinking little about the consequences of actually succeeding in his objective. Once he got hold of the panicked bird, it predictably began to scream and claw. Now in a panic himself, he threw it to the ground and stomped it to death.

The ancients thought the owl was a bad omen. In the year AD 77, Pliny the Elder said, "When it appears, it foretells nothing but evil." It was true for Walt Disney: that owl entered his dreams and haunted him for years. It created in him a morbid fear of death and colored even his many professional successes.

Disney's first big hit as a young animator came when he was twenty-six, in a cartoon featuring Mickey Mouse as Steamboat Willie. It had not only images but synchronized sound, effectively ending silent cinema and ensuring Disney's future as an entertainment pioneer. But he immediately followed it up with another short feature entitled "The Skeleton Dance," which opens with a terrified owl perched in a tree, followed by skeletons rising from their graves. Disney's distributor asked Roy, Walt's brother, "What's he trying to do, ruin us?" He went on, "You go back and tell that brother of yours the renters don't want this gruesome crap. . . . More mice, tell him. More mice!"[5]

This was a small sample of what was to come. As one scholar put it, "If Disney was a mouthpiece for an American way of life, the force of his voice depended on a curious obsession with death."[6] Virtually every one of his most famous films focused on the subject, from Snow White to Pinocchio.

His personal life was focused on decline and demise as well. According to his daughter Diane, he thought about it so much that in his early thirties, he hired a fortune-teller to predict when he would die. She told him he would perish at thirty-five—obviously the worst news he could receive. Workaholic and success addict that he was, to distract himself, he threw himself completely into his work. If he stayed busy, maybe he could distract both himself *and* the Reaper. He survived thirty-five but never forgot the prediction. Shortly before his fifty-fifth birthday, he mused that maybe he had misheard, and the fortune-teller had said *fifty-five*, not thirty-five.

Do you *really* want to go on forever?

Whenever someone asked my dad, "How's life?" he would cheerfully answer, "Better than the alternative!" If you live to work, you might give the same answer if someone asks, "How's work?"

When you think about it, however, dying isn't necessarily the inferior alternative. Jonathan Swift made this point in his 1726 novel *Gulliver's Travels*. In the nation of Luggnagg, the hero, Gulliver, finds a small group of people, born at random, called "struldbrugs." They look normal but are immortal. What luck! This is what Gulliver thinks until he learns that while they do not die, they do age and suffer the typical ailments of old people—the only difference being that the ailments are not lethal. They lose their eyesight and hearing and become senile but never die. At eighty, the government renders them legally dead and unable to own property or work. They live forever as unproductive wards of charity, horribly depressed and effectively invisible.[7]

This is fantasy in the case of physical death but a pretty accurate picture for many people in professional decline. Have you met people who refuse to accept the fact that they are past their prime—determined "to go until the wheels come off"? They consign themselves to frustration and miss out on opportunities to change and grow. At best, they might avoid being forced out of their jobs in humiliation but wind up as "professional struldbrugs": ineffective and treated with a weird combination of pity and contempt by others.

OK, you might be saying, so going on too long isn't such a great idea. What about leaving an amazing legacy—so at least you won't be forgotten? This is the "Achilles effect," from Homer's *Iliad*. He had to decide whether to fight in the Trojan War, promising certain physical death but a glorious legacy, or return to his home to live a long and happy life but die in obscurity. As he describes his choice,

two fates bear me on to the day of death.
If I hold out here and I lay siege to Troy,
my journey home is gone, but my glory never dies.
If I voyage back to the fatherland I love,
my pride, my glory dies."[8]

Achilles chooses the first option, giving him a mythic immortality that neither physical death nor decline could ever steal away.

The Achilles of the *Iliad* was an invention of Homer, but many think this way in real life. One of the most common strategies to avoid the agony of being forgotten is by trying to engineer a professional legacy. In my conversations for this book, many people in the end stages of their careers talked about how they wanted to be remembered.

But it doesn't work: *they forget you.* People move on. In the popular Jack Nicholson movie *About Schmidt*, the lead character is a retiring successful actuary, stunned to find that no one seeks out his advice; when he drops by the office to help out a few days after retirement, he finds them throwing all his old work in the dumpster. It's a scene with a lot of pathos, but it is based on truth. As one retired CEO told me as I was writing this book, "In just six months I went from 'Who's Who' to 'Who's He?'"

The Stoic philosopher and Roman emperor Marcus Aurelius reminds us that our efforts at posterity always fail, and thus are not worth pursuing. "Some indeed have not been remembered even for a short time, and others have become the heroes of fables, and again others have disappeared even from fables. Remember this then, that this little compound, thy-self, must either be dissolved, or thy poor breath must be extin-guished, or be removed and placed elsewhere."⁹ It's notable that Marcus's words have persisted for nearly two thousand years, so he is an exception to his own rule. But his point is still well taken, because you and I are no Marcus Aurelius. And sooner or later, even Marcus will disappear as well.

And do you really think—even if they do continue to vener-ate your legacy—that it will be so great? Remember the hero on the plane! It was the invidious contrast with his past fame and glory, momentarily enjoyable, that made his current status so bitter.

Finally, obsessing over the future squanders the present. I had an acquaintance who was extremely concerned with his professional reputation before death. Over the last few months of his life, when it was clear he was going to die soon, he spent most of his time finding ways to ensure he would be remem-bered for his accomplishments. If you love your work so much, you might as well enjoy it while you are doing it. If you spend time thinking about and working on your legacy, you are al-ready done.

The right way to think about your legacy

There is one way to leave a legacy that will help you live better right now. In his book *The Road to Character*, the writer David Brooks (a friend, but no relation) distinguishes between "ré-sumé virtues" and "eulogy virtues."¹⁰ Résumé virtues are professional and oriented toward earthly success. They require comparison with others. Eulogy virtues are ethical and spiritual and require no comparison. Your eulogy virtues are what you really would want people to talk about at your funeral. As in, "He was kind and deeply spiritual," and not, "He had a lot of frequent flier miles."

The striver's life makes it hard to focus on eulogy virtues. We want to be good people, of course, but focusing on eulogy virtues feels just so . . . *not special*. I have worked my whole career to do something better than everyone else—and I'm supposed to get distracted from that by doing things that *anybody* can do, like being nice?

But here's the thing: You lose your edge on those résumé skills, as everyone reading this book either knows or fears. Meanwhile, the eulogy virtues can get stronger and stronger, all the way up the crystallized intelligence curve and beyond. Practiced properly, old people have an edge over younger people, because they have more experience at life and relationships.

Furthermore, keeping and building your eulogy virtues is inherently rewarding. You won't be around to hear the eulogy—or for that matter, how people talk about you after retirement—but you will live the most fulfilling life by pursuing the virtues that are most personally valuable to you. Think how short-lived a professional reward—a promotion at work, say—is, compared with the fruits of generosity to a friend or family member. What gives you more satisfaction, an extra hour at work or an hour helping someone in need—or perhaps an hour in prayer?

Even if you are determined to build your eulogy virtues, the problem is that they keep getting crowded out by old habits and the daily grind. You don't quite get to that first hour listening to a friend because of that oh-so-pressing last hour of work.

A few sages give a clue on how to sort this out. According to Leo Tolstoy, "The worst thing about death is the fact that when a man is dead it is impossible any longer to undo the harm you have done him, or to do the good you haven't done him. They say: live in such a way as to be always ready to die. I would say: live in such a way that anyone can die without you having anything to regret."[11]

In short, imagine it's your last year of life, as well as of work. On the Sunday afternoon before the first day of each month, contemplate these questions: If I had one year left in my career and my life, how would I structure this coming month? What would be on my to-do list? What would I choose not to worry about? I am willing to guess that "taking an extra work trip at the expense of seeing my spouse" and "staying late to impress the boss" are not items that will be on your schedule. More likely, "take a weekend away" and "call my friend" will show up instead.

This discipline helps us work on *mindfulness*—living in the present as opposed to the past or future—which studies consistently find leads us to be happier people. But it also helps us to make the decisions that truly expose our best selves.

Tackling decline head-on

To contemplate your eulogy, however, is the easy part. Now the harder part: staring right at your death and decline itself. This is what will truly eradicate the fear.

There's really nothing novel about this advice. If you were morbidly afraid of snakes and went to a therapist, the most likely course of treatment would be . . . snakes. Exposure therapy has been firmly established as the best way to take on fears and phobias.[12] The reason is what psychologists call "desensitization," in which repeated exposure to something repellent or frightening makes it seems ordinary, prosaic, and certainly not scary.

If it works with snakes, it can work with death and decline. In 2017, a team of researchers at several American universities recruited volunteers to imagine they were terminally ill or on death row and then write fictional blog posts about their imagined feelings. The researchers then compared those posts with writings by those who were actually dying or facing capital punishment. The results, published in *Psychological Science*, were stark: the writing of those temporarily imagining death was three times as negative as that of those actually facing it—suggesting that, counterintuitively, death becomes scarier when it is abstract and remote than when it is a concrete reality.[13]

The research is modern, but the concept isn't. In the words of sixteenth-century French essayist Michel de Montaigne, "To begin depriving death of its greatest advantage over us, let us deprive death of its strangeness, let us frequent it, let us get used to it; let us have nothing more often in mind than death."[14]

But exposure does more than just defeat fear. Contemplating death can even make life more meaningful. As the novelist E. M. Forster put it, "Death destroys a man: the idea of

Death saves him."⁵ Why? Simply put, scarcity makes everything dearer to us. Remembering that life won't last forever makes us enjoy it all the more today.

It is a great irony about succeeding in the modern world that those who specialize in dominating fear—who rise to any challenge, concede no weakness, and meet any foe—are often desperately afraid of decline. But within this very irony resides a magnificent opportunity to beat fear once and for all and thus truly to be the person you have made yourself out to be.

If you ever visit Theravada Buddhist monasteries in Thailand and Sri Lanka, you will notice that many display photos of corpses in various states of decomposition. At first, it seems morbid and disturbing. As we now know, however, it is simply good psychology: it is exposure therapy. "This body, too," Buddhist monks are taught to say about their own bodies, "such is its nature, such is its future, such its unavoidable fate."

This is a meditation called *maranasati* (mindfulness of death), in which the practitioner imagines nine states of his or her own dead body:

1. A swollen corpse, blue and festering
2. Being eaten by scavengers and worms
3. Bones held together with some pieces of flesh and tendons
4. Blood-smeared bones without flesh but held together with tendons
5. Bones held together with tendons

6. Loose bones
7. Bleached bones
8. Bones more than a year old, in a pile
9. Bones that have turned to dust

Like resistance to death, resistance to the decline in your abilities is futile. And futile resistance brings unhappiness and frustration. Resisting your decline will bring you misery and distract you from life's opportunities. We should not avoid the truth. We should stare right at it; contemplate it; consider it; meditate on it. I practice a version of *maranasati*, in which I mindfully envision each of the following states:

1. I feel my competence declining
2. Those close to me begin to notice that I am not as sharp as I used to be
3. Other people receive the social and professional attention I used to receive
4. I have to decrease my workload and step back from daily activities I once completed with ease
5. I am no longer able to work
6. Many people I meet do not recognize me or know me for my previous work
7. I am still alive, but professionally I am no one
8. I lose the ability to communicate my thoughts and ideas to those around me
9. I am dead, and I am no longer remembered at all for my accomplishments

There is a famous Zen Buddhist story about a band of samurai who ride through the countryside causing destruction and terror. As they approach a monastery, all the monks scatter in fear, except for the abbot, a man who has completely mastered the fear of his own death. The samurai enter to find him sitting in the lotus position in perfect equanimity. Drawing his sword, the leader snarls, "Don't you see that I am the sort of man who could run you through without batting an eye?" The master responds, "Don't you see that I am a man who could be run through without batting an eye?"

The true master, when his or her prestige is threatened by age or circumstance, can say, "Don't you see that I am a person who could be utterly forgotten without batting an eye?"

One key difference between death and decline

"There's no greater misfortune than dying alone," wrote the Colombian novelist Gabriel García Márquez.[16] What he meant of course was dying with no one at your side, which does indeed seem a tragedy. But of course, we all make the *passage* of death alone. As they always say about your possessions, "You can't take it with you." But they could just as well mean your friends and family, as far as we know. That's one of the reasons people find it so frightening.

But this is where the parallel between death and decline stops. With decline, you don't have to experience it alone. In fact, you shouldn't. The problem is that many people *do* decline alone: on their way up they have let their relationships wither, so on the way down they don't have a human safety net. This makes any change in the second half seem all the more difficult and risky.

We can fix this, though, and it's our next chapter.

CHAPTER 6

Cultivate Your Aspen Grove

I think that I shall never see
A poem lovely as a tree.
JOYCE KILMER, 1913[1]

IT WAS A BEAUTIFUL COLORADO summer day in 2018, and I was in the early stages of thinking about this book. I was sitting under a stately aspen tree, with its leaves shimmering in the June breeze.

A tree is a perfect metaphor for a truly successful person, it seemed to me. Trees are strong, durable, reliable, and solid. As the book of Psalms describes a person who has achieved righteousness, "And he shall be like a tree planted by the rivers of water, that bringeth forth his fruit in his season; his leaf also shall not wither; and whatsoever he doeth shall prosper."[2]

Strong, productive—and ruggedly individual. Whether one of a million in a forest or standing by itself on the savannah, a tree grows silently on its own, reaches its own heights, and ultimately dies alone. Right?

Wrong. The aspen tree, it turns out, is not a solitary majesty, as I learned by sheer coincidence later that day from a friend who knows a lot more about trees than I do. He explained to me that each "individual" tree forms part of an enormous root system. In fact, the aspen is the largest living organism in the world; one stand of aspens in Utah called "Pando" spans 106 acres and weighs *6 million kilograms*.

That "lone" aspen I was looking at was no such thing. It was simply one shoot up from a vast root system—one expression among many of the same plant.

That got me to wondering whether the aspen was a special case. Later in the summer I found myself in Northern California, in the redwood forest. The giant redwoods—*Sequoiadendron giganteum*—are the most massive individual trees on earth. Not a single system like the aspens; maybe this was a better metaphor for the rugged individual?

Again: no. The redwood, which can grow to 275 feet tall, has remarkably shallow roots—often only 5 or 6 feet deep. It seems to violate the laws of physics that they can stay upright for hundreds—even thousands—of years. That is, until you know one more fact: the redwoods grow in thick groves because their shallow roots are intertwined and, over time, fuse together. They start out as individuals and become one with others as they mature and grow.

The aspen and the redwood are almost perfect metaphors for the Buddhist belief that the "self" is actually an illusion. We are all intertwined, Buddhist thinking goes, and our "individual" lives are simply manifestations of a more holistic life force. Ignoring this, the Buddhists feel, leads to living in an illusion and a lot of suffering. As Buddhist monk and writer Matthieu Ricard puts it, "Our grasping to the perception of a 'self' as a separate entity leads to an increasing feeling of vulnerability and insecurity. It also reinforces self-centeredness, mental rumination, and thoughts of hope and fear, and distances ourselves from others. This imagined self becomes the constant victim hit by life's events."[3]

No matter your religious views, the point is helpful and instructive: humans are naturally interconnected—biologically, emotionally, psychologically, intellectually, and spiritually. Creating an isolated self is dangerous and damaging because it is unnatural. Just as seeing only the one aspen is a misunderstanding of its true nature, the lone person—no matter how strong, accomplished, and successful—is a misunderstanding of ours as well.

We may look solitary, but we form a vast root system of families, friends, communities, nations, and indeed the entire world. The inevitable changes in my life—and yours—aren't a tragedy to regret. They are just changes to one interconnected member of the human family—one shoot from the root system. The secret to bearing my decline—no, enjoying it—is to be more conscious of the roots linking me to others. If I am connected to others in love, my decrease will be more than offset by increases to others—which is to say, increases to other facets of my true self.

Further, my connection to others makes my jump to the second curve all the more natural and normal. Indeed, the crystallized intelligence curve is predicated on interconnectedness. Without it, my wisdom has no outlet.

Establishing a root system isn't always simple, though. Many strivers have spent their adult lives under the illusion of their solitariness and now suffer the result. Their root systems are withered and unhealthy. Less metaphorically, they are simply *lonely*. The lessons in this chapter focus on how to build—or rebuild—a proper root system. We will first look at the evidence on love and happiness, especially in the second half of life. Then we will take on the loneliness that so many successful people feel and how to meet it head-on.

Omnia vincit amor

In 1938, researchers at Harvard Medical School lit upon a crazy but visionary idea: They would sign up a bunch of men then studying at Harvard and follow them over their whole adult lives, until they died. They would question them every year along the way about their lifestyles, habits, relationships, work, and happiness. Even though the original researchers would all be dead and gone, in a few decades, new researchers would be able to see how what people do early in life relates to how well—or poorly—they age.[4]

And thus, the Harvard Study of Adult Development was born. The original cohort of 268 men included people from many walks of life, including some who went on to become well-known, such as John F. Kennedy and *Washington Post* editor Ben Bradlee. Still, over the decades it was deemed too demographically insular—all Harvard men!—to give generalizable results, so it was paired with another dataset (called the Glueck Study) that had been tracking 456 disadvantaged youths from Boston starting at about the same time. Together, these data have been updated continually for more than eighty years. Fewer than sixty of the original participants are still alive, and the study is now tracking children and grandchildren of the first generation.

The result of this study is like a crystal ball of happiness: you look at how people lived, loved, and worked in their twenties and thirties, and then you can see how their lives turned out over the following decades. The longtime study director, Harvard psychiatry professor George Vaillant, wrote three best-selling books on the results. His successor, psychiatry professor Robert Waldinger, popularized the study even more with a viral TED Talk, "What Makes a Good Life? Lessons from the Longest Study on Happiness," which has been viewed nearly forty million times.

One of the most interesting things that the researchers have done over the years is categorize the participants when old with respect to happiness and health. The best off were called "Happy-Well," who enjoyed six dimensions of good physical health, as well as good mental health and high life satisfaction. On the very other end of the spectrum were the "Sad-Sick," who were below average in physical health, mental health, and life satisfaction.[5]

What led to being in each category? This is the million-dollar question for all of us, isn't it? The researchers found that some of the predictors are controllable, while others aren't.

Among the uncontrollable factors—uncontrollable by us, at least—are the social class of parents, having a happy childhood, having long-lived ancestors, and avoiding clinical depression. Not very surprising or useful information there.

Much more useful are the factors we *can* influence and that matter a great deal for late-life wellness. There are seven big predictors of being Happy-Well that we can control pretty directly:[6]

1. Smoking. Simple: don't smoke—or at least, quit early.

2. Drinking. Alcohol abuse is one of the most obvious factors in the Grant Study leading to Sad-Sick and putting Happy-Well out of reach. If there is *any* indication of problem drinking in your life, or if you have drinking problems in your family, do not wonder about it or take your chances. Quit drinking right now.

3. Healthy body weight. Avoid obesity. Without being fanatical, maintain a body weight in the normal range, eating in a moderate, healthy way without yo-yo dieting or crazy restrictions you can't maintain over the long run.

4. Exercise. Stay physically active, even with a sedentary job. Arguably the single best, time-tested way to do this is walking every day. (More on that later.)

5. Adaptive coping style. That means confronting problems directly, appraising them honestly, and dealing with them directly without excessive

      rumination, unhealthy emotional reactions, or
      avoidance behavior.

6. Education. More education leads to a more active mind later on, and that means a longer, happier life. That doesn't mean going to Harvard; it simply means lifelong, purposive learning, and lots of reading.

7. Stable, long-term relationships. For most, this is a steady marriage, but there are other relationships that can fit here. The point is having people with whom you grow together, whom you can count on, no matter what comes your way.

Seven goals isn't so many, but it is handy to know the most important *one thing* to remember. That boiling-down process can be extremely helpful to focus the mind. Is it the smoking, drinking, or exercise?

No. According to George Vaillant, the single most important trait of Happy-Well elders is healthy relationships. As he puts it, "Happiness is love. Full stop."[7] He elaborates a little: "There are two pillars of happiness. . . . One is love. The other is finding a way of coping with life that does not push love away."[8] And just for good measure, he quotes Virgil: *"Omnia vincit amor":* Love conquers all.

Vaillant's successor, Robert Waldinger, puts it this way: "The lessons aren't about wealth or fame or working harder and harder. The clearest message that we get from this . . . study is this: good relationships keep us happier and healthier. Period." Further, "The people who were the most satisfied in their relationships at age fifty were the healthiest at age eighty."

All the lonely people

Just focus on love! Sounds simple, doesn't it? It isn't, not for a lot of people, especially strivers who have worked their whole lives for worldly success but whose relationships have withered over the years and who are now quite isolated.

Loneliness is not the same as being alone, of course, because one can be emotionally and socially connected to others while alone. In fact, being alone is critical to one's emotional well-being and peace of mind. Some people—not me, but one of my kids, for example—are happiest by themselves, as long as they have healthy social and emotional connections. The theologian and philosopher Paul Tillich put it like this in his classic book *The Eternal Now*: "Solitude expresses the glory of being alone, whereas loneliness expresses the pain of feeling alone."[9]

Loneliness is the experience of emotional and social isolation. It has the weird property of being utterly ubiquitous yet feeling completely unique. The novelist Thomas Wolfe wrote in his essay "God's Lonely Man," "The whole conviction of my life now rests upon the belief that loneliness, far from being a rare and curious phenomenon, is the central and inevitable fact of human existence."[10] Lonely people feel like they are the only ones who feel lonely. They feel lonely in their very loneliness.

Just because it is common, however, doesn't mean loneliness is harmless. Research has established that the stress it creates leads to lowered immunity to disease, insomnia, cognitive sluggishness, and higher blood pressure.[11] Lonely people tend toward high-calorie, high-fat diets and lead more sedentary lives than non-lonely people. In her book *The Lonely Century*, Noreena Hertz shows that in terms of health outcomes, loneliness is comparable to smoking fifteen cigarettes per day and is worse than obesity.[12] It is also strongly associated with cognitive decline and dementia.

No surprise, then, that health officials are taking notice of loneliness as a public health threat. U.S. surgeon general Vivek Murthy has written a book about this, which starts with these words: "During my years caring for patients, the most common condition I saw was not heart disease or diabetes; it was loneliness."[13] And indeed, one doctor I interviewed for this book told me that he has longtime patients—often very successful people—who come to him basically just to have someone to talk to with whom they can be completely honest.

The U.S. Health Resources and Services Administration has declared a "loneliness epidemic," specifically citing the increasing phenomena of "no participation in social groups, fewer friends, and strained relationships" as the culprits.[14] For health care companies, loneliness is driving up costs. The insurance company Cigna has devoted significant resources to understanding why social isolation is increasing, finding that in 2018, 46 percent of Americans felt alone, and 43 percent of Americans felt that their relationships were not meaningful.[15]

Not everyone suffers equally from loneliness, of course. Some have a natural proclivity for it. Others have life circumstances that would make them more isolated than others. While gender and age aren't good predictors, marital status matters:

married people are less lonely than those who are divorced, widowed, and never married. However, loneliest of all are those who are married but with an "absent spouse." (Workaholics, take note: your spouse is probably lonely—and suffering as a result.)

And retirement? I have looked into whether people get lonelier after they retire and found that some do, but only those who tended toward loneliness to begin with.[16] In other words, the kind of people who don't know how to manage social interactions outside of work get lonelier when they retire. That describes a lot of successful people I know.

You might wonder which jobs and careers are the loneliest. It makes sense that you would find lonely people in professions where people spend a lot of time by themselves. I thought about farmers, for example. After high school, one of my sons took a job farming wheat in Idaho, and I remember that during harvest, he would spend fourteen hours a day alone in a combine. At other times, he would be by himself all day, fixing fences and picking boulders out of the soil. He was almost always alone. But my son—who is highly social—never complained about feeling lonely. And in fact, his off-hours were nearly always spent with his friends and the family who owned the farm.

Then I thought about people in sales. Hotel to hotel, airport to airport—it has to be horribly lonely, right? It turns out neither farmers nor traveling salespeople are on the list of loneliest jobs. The top two loneliest professions, according to the *Harvard Business Review,* are lawyers and doctors.[17] Both of these are high-skill, high-pay, high-prestige professions . . . maybe something like yours.

The lonely leader

Earlier we talked about the fact that successful, upwardly mobile people are the ones most prone to suffering when their skills start to decline. It surprises people to hear this, but it shouldn't: after all, the bigger they are, the harder they fall.

A similar principle applies to loneliness, which is a special malady for people who have enjoyed a lot of worldly success. Sometimes examples of this are celebrities known to all of us but close to no one. Take celebrity chef Anthony Bourdain, for example. I was always kind of a fan of his. Not that I care so much about food; I just thought his television shows, *No Reservations* and *Parts Unknown*, were exquisitely beautiful and was amazed how he used something as prosaic as eating to introduce viewers to the world. "What a fun life he must have," I thought. And indeed, "I have the best job in the world," he told *The New Yorker* in an interview. "If I'm unhappy, it's a failure of imagination."[18]

You probably know where I'm going here. On June 8, 2018, Bourdain hanged himself in a hotel room in France, where he was filming an episode of his show. I didn't know much about Bourdain's private life. Out of professional (rather than prurient) interest, I read articles about what might have contributed to the self-destruction of someone who seemed to have it all. In the explanations that emerged—he had a drinking problem, he had relationship issues, and so forth—the two characteristics I saw over and over again were his workaholism and what one author called his "unfathomable loneliness."[19] Bourdain worked brutally long hours, year after year. He was always surrounded by others but, by all accounts, connected at a deep human level with very few.

But it isn't just world-famous people who wind up feeling isolated and lonely. Plenty of ordinary high achievers do as well. Wrapped up in their fear of falling behind, success-addicted workaholics—like all people controlled by their addictive behavior—leave little room in their lives for friends or family. As the late John Cacioppo, a University of Chicago social neuroscientist and pioneer in the study of loneliness, put it, "Loneliness reflects how you feel about your relationships."[20] So even though they may be in a family or a crowded workplace, workaholics *feel* all alone, except for their terrible, beloved work.

Leaders are particularly prone to loneliness, in no small part because real friendships at work are difficult or impossible with people under one's authority and supervision. Work friendships are so important that 70 percent of people say friendship at work is the most important element to a happy work life, and 58 percent say they would turn down a higher-paying job if it meant not getting along with coworkers.[21] According to a data analysis conducted by Gallup in 2020, employees who say they have a best friend at work are almost twice as likely as others to enjoy their workday and almost 50 percent more likely to report high social well-being.

But people at the top often miss out on true workplace friendships and suffer mightily as a result. According to one finding in the *Harvard Business Review*, for example, half of CEOs experience loneliness on the job, and most of them feel loneliness hinders their work performance.[22] Studies also have shown that loneliness is linked to burnout among leaders.[23]

Loneliness at the top doesn't come from physical isolation—who spends more time in meetings than a CEO?—but from an inability to make deep human connections at work as a result of the leader's position. At work, successful people are lonely in a crowd.

A study by Princeton psychologist Daniel Kahneman and colleagues provides a clue as to why leaders are isolated. The researchers asked a large group of working women to reconstruct their day to ascertain the moments that yielded the highest levels of positive and negative emotion.[24] The positive side of the ledger yielded few surprises: The top three activities were, in order: sex, socializing, and relaxing. The top three happiness-inducing interaction partners were friends, relatives, and spouse (which seem out of order, given the activities list, but no matter). The top three activities for producing negative feelings were working, childcare, and commuting (sorry, kids). The second and third most negative interaction partners were clients and coworkers. But the top spot for negative interactions? The boss. No one wants to hang around with the lonely boss.

That explained a lot for me, especially after I started digging deeper into the reasons. One famous study from 1972 found that subordinates in a workplace tend to lose their sense of free will about being friends with the boss—you are unfriendly to her or him at your peril—which makes things uncomfortable and weird.[25] More recent research has shown that subordinates objectify leaders by seeing them not as people per se, but as dispensers of power, information, and money.[26]

But even if employees don't endow the boss with negative qualities, they can make the relationship awkward and unfun. One study from 2003 found that subordinates in the workplace often treat their superiors like authority figures from their childhood, such as parents or teachers. Even if they don't refer to the boss as "Mommy," this makes peer-to-peer friendship impossible and leaves the boss, who might be a former colleague, socially alone.[27]

People with authority isolate themselves as well. The authors of the famous 1950 book *The Lonely Crowd* claimed that leaders are lonely because their success requires manipulation and persuasion of others.[28] As such, they objectify subordinates every bit as much as subordinates objectify them. Later research found that leaders often purposely distance themselves from employees so they can appraise their performance fairly.[29] In plain terms, if you might have to fire someone, you are unlikely to form tight bonds with that person.

Romance and friendship

The relationships that best mitigate loneliness—the aspens closest to us that we need to cultivate—are romantic partnerships and close friendships. Let's take a look at each, and then see why strivers so often neglect them.

There is a lot of research on why some romantic relationships are stable and others are not. It is well-known that a big percentage of all marriages in the United States end in divorce or separation (about 39 percent, according to the latest data).[30]

But staying together is not what really counts. Analysis of the Harvard Study data shows that marriage per se accounts for only 2 percent of subjective well-being later in life.[31] The important thing for health and well-being is relationship satisfaction.

Popular culture would have you believe the secret to this satisfaction is romantic passion, but that is wrong. On the contrary, a lot of unhappiness can attend the early stages of romance. For example, researchers find that it is often accompanied by rumination, jealousy, and "surveillance behaviors"—not what we typically associate with happiness. Furthermore, "destiny beliefs" about soul mates or love being *meant to be* can predict low forgiveness when paired with attachment anxiety.[32] Romance often hijacks our brains in a way that can cause the highs of elation or the depths of despair.[33] You might accurately say that falling in love is the start-up cost for happiness—an exhilarating but stressful stage we have to endure to get to the relationships that actually fulfill us.

The secret to happiness isn't falling in love; it's *staying* in love, which depends on what psychologists call "companionate love"—love based less on passionate highs and lows and more on stable affection, mutual understanding, and commitment.[34] You might think "companionate love" sounds a little, well, disappointing. I certainly did the first time I heard it, on the heels of great efforts to win my future wife's love. But over the past thirty years, it turns out that we don't just love each other; we *like* each other, too. Once and always my romantic love, she is also my best friend.

Being rooted in friendship is the reason that companionate

love creates true happiness.[35] Passionate love, which relies on attraction, does not typically last beyond the novelty stage of the relationship. Companionate love relies on its very familiarity. As one researcher bluntly summarizes the evidence in the *Journal of Happiness Studies*, "The well-being benefits of marriage are much greater for those who also regard their spouse as their best friend."[36] This is the kind of love that perseveres across crises, over time, and thus that delivers the Happy-Well benefits.

Best friends get enjoyment, satisfaction, and meaning from each other's company. They bring out the best in each other; they gently tease each other; they have fun together. President Calvin Coolidge and his wife, Grace, famously had such a friendship. According to one story (perhaps apocryphal), when the president and first lady were touring a poultry farm, Mrs. Coolidge remarked to the farmer—loud enough for the president to hear—that it was amazing so many eggs were fertilized by just one rooster.[37] The farmer told her that the roosters did their jobs over and over again each day. "Perhaps you could point that out to Mr. Coolidge," she told him with a smile. The president, noting the remark, inquired whether the rooster serviced the same hen each time. No, the farmer told him, there were many hens for each rooster. "Perhaps you could point that out to Mrs. Coolidge," said the president.

Promiscuous roosters notwithstanding, the romance of companionate love seems to make people happiest when it's monogamous. I say this as a social scientist, not a moralist: in 2004, a survey of sixteen thousand American adults found that for men and women alike, "the happiness-maximizing number of sexual partners in the previous year is calculated to be 1."[38]

Your romantic partnership is arguably your most important relationship. However, it is neither necessary nor sufficient to prevent loneliness. Robert Waldinger has told me that, in fact, he sees no difference in happiness between senior citizens who are married and those who remained single that owes to the marriage per se. You can be single and happy if you have other close, fulfilling family links and friendships.

But, equally important, your marriage cannot be your only true friendship. In 2007, researchers at the University of Michigan looked at married people aged twenty-two to seventy-nine who said they had close friends.[39] Having at least two—meaning at least one not being the spouse—was associated with higher levels of life satisfaction, self-esteem, and lower levels of depression. For those who can't name two, the spousal relationship was much more important for meeting emotional needs, and this can lead to problems. It is a lot of pressure on a marriage to fill almost every emotional role and makes rough patches in a marriage all the more catastrophic and isolating.

My father's only truly close friend was my mother. He was an introvert, and intimate friendships came with great difficulty, so this was the path of least resistance. And they had a good marriage: their wedding came four days after they graduated from college and lasted forty-four years, until his death at age sixty-six.

But having your spouse or partner as your one and only close friend is imprudent, like having a radically undiversified investment portfolio. If something goes wrong in your marriage, you can be left single *and* without friends. That is often the case when a couple divorces or when a spouse dies.

Many older adults figure this out as they age and build a non-spouse friend network. This is especially true for women, who have larger, denser, more supportive friend networks than men.[40] And they are very gender-sorted networks: apart from their husbands, older women rarely even consider men as *friends*—only a fifth of older women name a male friend in their list of intimates.

All this is important for older men to understand if they find their wives turning outward for friendship. Marriage bonds are more emotionally important to men as they age than they are to older women, because for many men, work has crowded out friendships, and those they have are more focused on, say, golf than feelings.[41] Their wives have invested elsewhere for emotional support, which frankly is prudent and wise.

Some people assume that as they age, their intimate relationships will be built around their adult children. After all, these are the relationships in which we have invested the most—literally and figuratively. They know us, and we know them—I look at my kids and it is like looking into my own twenty-something soul! Shouldn't they be my best friends as I age?

Probably not. I find that most of the conflict I have with my adult kids stems from my own poor memory of my relationship with my own parents. They were good parents, but I wanted my independence. It was important to me to have a certain amount of separation, not from bitterness but because I wanted to build my own life. And so it is with my kids: our relationship is great, but they are focused on their lives, not mine—as they should be. For this reason, the research finds that contact with unrelated friends is more strongly correlated with well-being than contact with adult children.[42] As two scholars on friendship put it, "Interaction with family members is often dictated by obligation, whereas interaction with friends is primarily motivated by pleasure."[43]

Do you have *real* friends—or *deal* friends?

I remember years ago, I was on a fishing trip with my son Carlos in Florida. He was twelve or thirteen years old, and the trip was his Christmas present—he asked for the same thing every year: a trip to Florida to hunt and fish, just the two of us. We did it every year for a decade, until he joined the Marines (and he promises we will start doing it again when he leaves the military—as *my* Christmas present).

We were just setting out on Lake Okeechobee early Saturday morning to catch some largemouth bass, when my mobile phone rang. I checked the caller ID and saw it was the head of a large foundation with which I was doing a deal in my capacity as president of my nonprofit organization. "I have to take this," I told Carlos and sat in the car talking to the other man. The first five minutes were small talk about his family and mine, even though we weren't personally close. Then we got down to business.

After I hung up, Carlos asked who that was. "A friend," I answered. Which was technically true—we liked each other well enough and were on a first-name basis. I had had dinner with him socially once. Carlos looked at me with the look he always gives me when he thinks I am full of it.

"A real friend, or a *deal* friend?" he asked.

Clever boy. I stopped short. He was on the money of course—our kids know us shockingly well. But I asked him what he meant anyway. "You don't have very many real friends," he said. "You know lots of important people, though, and you do each other favors. Those are deal friends, not real friends."

Without being aware of it, Carlos was making a distinction in relationships that Aristotle had made more than two thousand years earlier in his *Nicomachean Ethics*. Aristotle wrote that there is a kind of a friendship ladder, from lowest to highest. At the bottom—where emotional bonds are weakest and the benefits are lowest—are friendships based on utility: deal friends, to use Carlos's coinage. You are friends in an instrumental way, one that helps each of you achieve something else you want, such as professional success.

Higher up are friends based on pleasure. You are friends because of something you like and admire about the other person. They are entertaining, or funny, or beautiful, or smart, for example. In other words, you like an inherent quality, which makes it more elevated than a friendship of utility, but it is still basically instrumental.

At the highest level is Aristotle's "perfect friendship," which is based on willing each other's well-being and a shared love for something good and virtuous that is outside either of you. This might be a friendship forged around religious beliefs or passion for a social cause. What it isn't is *utilitarian*. The other person shares in your passion, which is intrinsic, not instrumental.

Of course, our friendships can be a blend. I can have a business partner whom I admire and who strongly shares my love for something good and virtuous. But I have found that in most cases, I can in fact classify my friendships pretty well into Aristotle's three baskets, and my utility basket tends to be fullest.

Carlos's question made me reflect on the fact that, like a lot of hardworking, ambitious people, I had lots and lots of "deal friends" but not too many real friends, and I was pretty lonely as a result. I vowed to cultivate my few real friendships much more.

And what about you? Do you have real friends—or just deal friends? It matters a lot for your happiness. In 2018, researchers at the University of California, Los Angeles, fielded a survey about loneliness, in which they asked how often they feel like no one knows them well.[44] Fifty-four percent said they feel that way "always" or "sometimes." Does this include you? Before you answer, name two or three real friends. If you are married, take out your spouse. Now, be honest: When was the last time you talked to each of these "real friends" in depth? Would you be comfortable calling them if you were in trouble?

If you struggled to name two or three, there's a problem. And if you haven't talked to them in a few months, or wouldn't call them in a crisis, you are most likely mixing up real friends with deal friends. Not that you are being untruthful—you might simply have not cultivated real friendships in a long, long time.

Building real friendships can be tricky for people who haven't done so for many years—maybe since childhood. Researchers find it is often harder for men than women.[45] Furthermore, women generally base friendships on social and emotional support, whereas men are more likely to base friendships on shared activities, including work. In other words, women have more real friends; men have more deal friends.[46]

This matters a lot for well-being, especially later in life. Numerous studies have shown that one of the great markers for happiness among people at midlife and beyond is people who can rattle off the names of a few authentic, close friends.[47] It is not necessary that they be numerous to achieve happiness, and, in fact, people tend to get more selective about their friends as they age and reduce the number of true intimates.[48] But the number of real friends needs to be more than zero and more than just your spouse.

Recognizing these patterns, I resolved to make closer friends, and my wife vowed to collaborate. This is not easy for anyone, and especially hard for me because we have moved a lot, so my friendships where I live don't have roots that go back years. So we devised a plan: we started organizing our social life specifically around conversations about profound issues. At the risk of becoming Mr. and Mrs. Intense, we directed dinnertime chats with friends away from trivialities like vacation plans and house purchases and toward issues of happiness, love, and spirituality. This deepened some of our friendships and in other cases showed us that a more fulfilling relationship wasn't going to be possible—and, thus, where to put less energy.

The barriers to love

Here's the bottom-line summary about your relationships—the key points for cultivating your aspen grove:

- You need strong human connections to help you get on the second curve and flourish.
- No matter how introverted you are, you cannot expect to thrive into old age without healthy, intimate relationships.
- For married people, a loving, companionate spousal relationship is key to thriving.
- Marriage and family are not an adequate substitute for close friendships, which should not be left up to chance.
- Friendship is a skill that requires practice, time, and commitment.
- Work friendships are not a substitute for real friendships, although they can also be satisfying, if designed purposively.

In my interviews and conversations over the past several years, I find a surprising amount of resistance to this information and the advice to start building relationships immediately. Here are three things people often tell me.

"I just don't have time."

Love and friendships are enormously time-consuming, it's

true. They crowd out all kinds of other things, like . . . well, let's be honest: for many readers of this book, they mostly crowd out *work*. If that's the case for you, and it's what is holding back the proper development of romance, parenting, and real friendships, you have your priorities unbalanced.

Remember, a classic sign of addictive behavior is when something not human starts to supplant human relationships. Hence the term "workaholism," which we discussed earlier—the all-consuming need to work, achieve, earn, and succeed. If you are displaying workaholic behavior, no amount of advice about making friends will help. You will never have time or energy left for close relationships. You need to address the workaholism problem before anything else.

Acknowledging this truth requires facing what the workaholic is avoiding with the extra hour of work. If it is dysfunctional relationships themselves—possibly brought on by years of neglect—it will only get worse by indulging the addiction. It is worth remembering that the cliché image of an old man on his deathbed saying to his family "I wish I'd spent more time at work" is a *joke*. To escape his addiction, the workaholic has to reapportion time and use it to establish or reestablish friendships and family life.

This leads to the second lament I often hear, once the problem has been acknowledged:

"My relationships are so withered, I don't know where to start."

Some have gone many years without cultivating close relationships with others. The ties with family members and "friends" are not the only problem after years of neglect, however. Arguably a bigger problem is that closeness requires practice. You can basically lose your "love chops" if you neglect them for a long time.

If that describes you, you will need to reawaken your dormant relationship skills. The first step is articulating your desire for deeper connections. This signals to others your commitment to change—but more important, it signals this commitment to yourself. Often, change is just an idea in our heads until we say it out loud. I have known people who have been "thinking about" a life change for decades. Thinking about working less and spending more time with family and friends isn't worth much. But telling your loved ones you want this will program the ideas into your brain and set you toward meeting this goal.

But how do you get started when you've lost your skills? Is a sixty-five-year-old businessman just supposed to call another guy and suggest a playdate? Ridiculous!

Actually . . . maybe not so ridiculous. I remember when my kids were really little, we would get them together with other children. They wouldn't exactly play together; they would do something child development experts call "parallel play": the kids play with their own toys individually, but next to each other. This is part of their process of acquiring friendship skills. Little by little, they start interacting more, until over the months that pass, they wind up playing together with the same toys.

There is a new phenomenon emerging in several countries including the United States, United Kingdom, and Australia, called "Men's Sheds." It is basically parallel play for older men who are relearning friendship skills.[49] Men who are lonely—many retired, but not all—are left by their loved ones in, well, sheds full of woodworking tools where they can work on crafts projects in parallel with other men. Remember, men tend to develop friendships in the course of shared activities, and these crafts allow this while not requiring direct collaboration—parallel play. Little by little, the men begin to interact with one another, rebuilding friendship skills as they make new friends. "I come here, I chat with people, and I feel like I accomplish something," one man told a *Washington Post* reporter while working on a football-shaped trophy for a friend. "I was nervous at first, but people were really welcoming, and now I come at least once a week."[50]

It doesn't really matter if it's sheds or something else. And for women who need to rebuild relationships, perhaps it's something else entirely. The point is that to kindle friendships requires acts, not intentions.

"I doubt people would forgive me."

In some cases, withered relationships feature a lot of ill will on the part of "loved" ones. Marriages have turned sour over decades of neglect, and the connections with adult children are ice-cold. Success addicts are often the object of tremendous resentment from people who needed and deserved their love and attention but did not receive it for many years.

It's time to make amends. Success addicts can learn a thing or two about recovery from alcoholics. Those who have followed the twelve-step program of Alcoholics Anonymous know that recovery is not possible without step 9: "[Make] direct amends to such people wherever possible, except when to do so would injure them or others." Alcoholics in recovery make a list of people they have hurt and neglected due to their addiction; they must make amends with each person on the list, if possible.

This is complicated, obviously. "Sorry I wrecked your car that night when I was drunk" might not heal a wound immediately or adequately. But it is a good start, especially when backed up by a commitment to refrain from drinking and repay the debt. And so it is for the victims of a success addiction. "Sorry about choosing tedious board meetings—which I don't even remember now—over your ballet recitals" probably won't fix everything. It has to be accompanied by new behavior. With relationships, actions speak louder than words, especially if your words have been fairly empty in the past.

Measuring your life

Earlier in this book I mentioned a question I ask my students to get their attention: How many Thanksgivings do you have left? The truth is that it gets my attention as well. If I follow suit with my parents, it's something like *eight*. (We Brookses die fairly young.) The point isn't to depress anybody. It is to remind us that in denominating time in memorable, scarce events, we have a much better sense of its scarcity. Thus, we use it more wisely. This is the same idea as saying we should live each day as if it were our last.

If we followed this insight, we would probably sort out our workaholism and success addiction problems. The cognitive error that feeds them is the idea that our time is limitless, so the marginal decision—what to do with the next hour—is not very important in the broad scheme of things. We come face-to-face with this error when time is up and it's too late.

This is what business management consultants might call a "systematic measurement error." And in that spirit, I have adopted the work of a business expert for an exercise to help me solve it in my life. The expert is the late Clayton Christensen, a longtime professor at the Harvard Business School, where I serve on the faculty. Christensen died a few months after I arrived at Harvard, but his legacy looms large at HBS, in no small part because of his famous book, *How Will You Measure Your Life?*[51]

Christensen analyzes a good life well lived in the same way he would assess a company, and the book is well worth reading in its entirety. However, one section provided me with the material for a three-part exercise for avoiding the snares of workaholism and success addiction, while investing in the relationships that bring true satisfaction.

1. ALLOCATE TIME WELL AHEAD OF TIME

Successful people are good at *marginal thinking*: making sure each hour is spent on its best use at that moment. The trouble is that this always marginalizes the things in life that don't have a clear payoff in the short run—like relationships. This is why an extra hour at work, even when we are exhausted and unproductive, can crowd out the first hour at home, day after day, year after year—leading to the problems of loneliness and alienation.

To avoid this error, I take an hour one Sunday afternoon

each month and start by imagining myself at the end of my life, surrounded by the people I love. I think about what they are saying about me.

Then I come back to the present. I think about how I want to allocate my time in the coming weeks. What do I want to do with my time this week to cultivate the relationships that will result in that end scenario? I might make the decision to leave work on time, leave my work at the office, get home for dinner, and watch a movie after dinner with my family.

2. DO YOUR CORE JOB

Many businesses fail because of what we might call the "Edsel problem," based on the famous 1958 car that Ford executives loved but that consumers hated. They sell what *they* like, rather than what the customer wants and needs. We can be like this in our relationships, especially when our competence has diminished after years of neglect. We give our families and friends the opportunity to spend time at *our* convenience, doing what is interesting to *us*. And it makes sense—if I am the king at work, I am the king at home!

It doesn't work this way, of course. Love relationships are not hierarchical, but reciprocal. They require giving what people want and need, not that which is most convenient to the giver.

I regularly write out a list of the people with whom I need a stronger relationship. Then I list next to each of them what they need from me that only I can provide. For example, there are things that only I can do for my wife. There are some things only I can do for my adult children. When those things are ne-glected, relationships starve.

3. INVEST INTELLIGENTLY

Once, when one of my sons was in high school, he asked me the three things I really wanted for him in life. I thought about it for a few days, and my own answer surprised me. I didn't say happiness, because while that's important, a good life of purpose and meaning also requires unhappiness. I certainly didn't say money or fame, as you can already predict. In the end, I told him, "Honesty, compassion, and faith." That's what I felt would make him the best man he could become.

After that, I decided to write down the three things I want for each of the people I love the most and then ask: Am I invest-ing in those things in their lives? Am I putting my time, energy, affection, expertise, and money toward the development of these assets and qualities? Am I modeling them with my own behav-ior? Do I need a new investment strategy?

The payoff

In 2009, researchers at the University of Rochester published a study in which they recruited 147 recent university gradu-ates and asked them their goals after graduation.[52] They found that goals fell into two basic categories, which they called "in-trinsic" and "extrinsic." Intrinsic goals centered around ful-fillment from deep, enduring relationships. Extrinsic goals centered on earning a lot of money, owning a lot of stuff, gaining power, or achieving reputation and fame—in other words, the wants that make up the denominator of the satisfaction equation. This is the stuff to toss out of the bucket.

The scholars followed up a year later to find out how the participants were doing. To begin with, people generally achieved their goals: those who wanted great relationships had them, while those who wanted money and power were on track to get those things. This is a pretty important finding: you are probably going to get what you wish for in life. This makes it all the more true, as the old saying goes, to "be careful what you wish for."

The second finding is the really profound one, though: people with intrinsic goals had happier lives after a year. Meanwhile, the people who pursued extrinsic goals experienced more negative emotions, such as shame and fear. They also suffered more physical maladies. In a nutshell, if your life goals revolve around lots of money, prestige, and other worldly things, you are setting yourself up to have exploding wants and low life satisfaction.

You kind of knew this, didn't you? Perhaps you have been a full-on extrinsic goals junkie for many years and have fed your addiction all the way up your fluid intelligence curve. But if you are mature and experienced in the ways of life—another way of saying you're getting up there in years, like me—you now know that extrinsic rewards are foolish goals. But it is precisely this knowledge that leads us to the frustrations of life. In your youth, you hold out hope that these haves *will* finally satisfy. As the years pass, you learn that they never do. But your habits are so ingrained, and you are so skilled at chasing the old rewards . . . You pursue a fading hope that if you finally have this or achieve that worldly goal, you will finally achieve the satisfaction you seek. This is an exercise in futility, and leaves you stuck on your declining fluid intelligence curve, the only place you know to look for rewards.

Only a shift to intrinsic goals will give you what you really want, and prepare you to get on the second curve, which requires relationships and sharing wisdom in the spirit of love. But can you get new goals, especially later in life? Indeed you can, but you need to state your intrinsic values more openly.

Here's a trick to get started on this: Visualize yourself at a party. Someone asks, "What do you do?" You answer not with extrinsic stuff like your job title, but with what you know will give you the most purpose, meaning, and joy. Involve your spiritual life, your relationships, and the way you serve others. Don't imagine yourself saying, "I'm a lawyer." Imagine yourself saying instead, "I'm a wife and a mother to three adult kids." Don't worry if you don't quite believe it yourself at first that this is who you truly are and what you do. You will speak this truth into existence in your life.

It's difficult to describe adequately the depth of the rewards that one enjoys when relationships become your "official" source of meaning and fulfillment. People compare it with finding buried treasure, with the only sadness being that it didn't happen earlier in life. Writers elegize the bliss of love and friendship. As Ralph Waldo Emerson wrote in his joyful essay "Friendship,"

I awoke this morning with devout thanksgiving for my
friends, the old and the new. Shall I not call God the
Beautiful, who daily showeth himself so to me in his
gifts? I chide society, I embrace solitude, and yet I am not
so ungrateful as not to see the wise, the lovely, and the
noble-minded, as from time to time they pass my gate.
Who hears me, who understands me, becomes mine—a
possession for all time.

An intimate friendship, whether it be from the companionate love of your spouse or an Aristotelian "perfect friend," is
better than any professional success. It will salve the wounds
of professional decline like nothing else.

Consider J. S. Bach, whom we met earlier. He loved his
work, and enjoyed his early success, but he knew what mattered
most. You don't become the loving father of twenty kids without
significant investment, and the well-documented warm relationships he had with both his wives and their surviving children indicate this investment was enormous. He loved them,
and they loved him. Bach's work and life were balanced in part
by blurring the line where one started and the other stopped.
His two-part inventions and sinfonias were written as exercises for their musical studies; his second wife was his copy-
ist; he was a major promoter of his children's musical careers.
The reason Bach died a happy man was not because of his success as a composer, which had decreased greatly over the last
decades of his life. It was because of the relationships he had
cultivated, which became the animating force behind his own

professional change from compositional innovator to master teacher.

Taking love even higher

I thought I was having a truly original insight that day under the aspen tree. But of course, many have seen this before me. The most notable is probably Henry David Thoreau, who wrote,

Two sturdy oaks I mean, which side by side,
Withstand the winter's storm,
And spite of wind and tide,
Grow up the meadow's pride,
For both are strong

Above they barely touch, but undermined
Down to their deepest source . . .
Admiring you shall find
Their roots are intertwined
Insep'rably.[53]

There is something inherently transcendent about relation-ships and the magical way they elevate us from our material drudgery, if we let them. Strivers have an incredible opportunity to pivot from struggling against the tide of professional decline toward the wellspring of joy that is the love of others as they move from the first to the second curve.

In truth, English is an impoverished language when it comes to love. In Greek, for example, there are several distinct words for love: *philia* (the love between friends), *eros* (romantic love), *storge* (the love by parents of children), *philautia* (self-love), and *xenia* (hospitality, or love of the stranger).

But the most transcendent of all the Greek concepts of love is *agape*: the love of man for the divine. It was regarded as the highest, most beatific kind of love. To achieve it is a kind of ecstasy. It doesn't come naturally to many strivers, however, who have put their faith for so long in themselves and the world's rewards. Our next lesson is how all of us can attain it, no matter where we are in our life's journey, and how it can give us the confidence to move forward with our lives.

CHAPTER 7

Start Your
Vanaprastha

It was a sticky, humid morning in February 2018 when I set off deep into the south Indian countryside. My destination was a small town called Palakkad, near the border between the states of Kerala and Tamil Nadu.

I should back up a bit. For years, since stumbling across the Hindu guru Paramahansa Yogananda's writings as a young man, I was aware of an ancient Indian theory of the *ashramas*, about how to transition through middle age in happiness and enlightenment. I didn't know much more than that, though. I googled around for it, looked for books in English, and asked Indian friends for details but never found much of any depth. This isn't too surprising, actually. A huge amount of deep Hindu philosophy has resisted the globalization of ideas and information. I had been told that to find what I was seeking, I needed to find a teacher.

Not that this search presented a hardship for me, mind you. For years I have been an Indiaphile. Since my first visit at age nineteen, I have loved the culture, the music, the food, the philosophy, and especially the Indians themselves. Between their sense of humor and easy spirituality, I always feel completely at home. I find an excuse to visit every year at least once, and I have sat at the feet of many a spiritual teacher on the subcontinent.

On that morning in 2018, I rose at four a.m. and traveled several hours by car to a small, unmarked home, where I hoped to meet the guru Sri Nochur Venkataraman. I had it on good authority that Venkataraman, known simply as "Acharya" ("Teacher") to his disciples, could explain to me the *ashramas* and, more specifically, who I should be looking to be as I head into the back half of life.

Obtaining a meeting with Acharya was no mean feat. Unlike many of the wealth- and fame-seeking guru-entrepreneurs in India, Acharya is not rich, seeks no media presence, and has never been to the West. He is a quiet, humble man dedicated to helping people attain spiritual growth. He has no interest in techies looking for clarity about a new start-up idea or Western dilettantes running away from their own religion. But with some cajoling, I convinced his retinue that I was neither shopping for a new faith nor out to make money.

The meeting was a scene made for television, although

there were no cameras. I removed my sandals and entered the unremarkable home, where I found the guru, surrounded by a circle of silent devotees. He made the traditional namaste greeting with his hands and said, "I've been waiting for you." We sat, and I was immediately filled with a complete sense of peace. For a few minutes, I forgot why I was there.

Recovering my focus, I told Acharya I had come in search of how to live life in its proper stages. Many people suffer as they age because they lose their abilities, gained over many years of hard work. Moving to a new stage of life is hard—even frightening. I had heard that he could give me insights into these matters.

Over the next two hours, Acharya explained the ancient Indian teaching that a proper life must be lived in four stages—these are the *ashramas*. Ideally, *ashramas* last twenty-five years each. Of course, that is generally not likely to occur; in America today, the odds of living to one hundred are only about one in six thousand; the odds are lower in India. But the deeper point of the wisdom is not to make it to one hundred and break life into equal parts; it is to spend significant time in each distinct stage.

The first *ashrama* is *brahmacharya*, the period of youth and young adulthood dedicated to learning. The second is *grihastha*, when a person builds a career, accumulates wealth, and maintains a family. This second stage seems fairly straightforward and uncontroversial, but in this stage the Hindu philosophers find one of life's most common traps: People become attached to its earthly rewards—money, power, sex, prestige—and thus try to make this stage last a lifetime. Sound familiar? This is another description of being stuck on the fluid intelligence curve, chasing Aquinas's four idols—money, power, pleasure, and honor—that lead to self-objectification, but that never satisfy.

To break the attachment to these idols requires movement to a new stage of life, with a new set of skills—spiritual skills. The change can be painful, Acharya said, like becoming an adult for a second time. And it means letting go of things that defined us in the eyes of the world. In other words, we have to move beyond the worldly rewards to experience transition and find wisdom in a new *ashrama*—and so defeat the scourge of attachments. That ordinarily occurs, if we are diligent, around age fifty.

And that new stage? It is called *vanaprastha*, which comes from two Sanskrit words meaning "retiring" and "into the forest."[1] This is the stage at which we purposively begin to pull back from our old personal and professional duties, becoming more and more devoted to spirituality and deep wisdom, crystallized intelligence, teaching, and faith. It does not mean the perfect life requires retiring at age fifty into a forest; rather, that one's life goals must readjust. *Vanaprastha* is the metaphysical context of the second curve.

But *vanaprastha* isn't the last stop, Acharya told me. That would be *sannyasa*, the last spiritual stage that comes in old age. This is the stage totally dedicated to the fruits of enlightenment. In times past, some Hindu men would literally leave their families around age seventy-five, take holy vows, and spend the rest of their lives at the feet of masters, praying and studying the holy scriptures. In Acharya's words, "The moment you realize the Self, you know that you are the Self, you are not the body. You know that you are the infinite Truth. That recognition, that realization is *sannyasa*."

Even if sitting in a cave at age seventy-five isn't your cup of tea, the point should still be clear. The goal of the last phase of life is to drink from the chalice of life's deepest secrets. But to be able to do that requires study and work on philosophical and theological matters, which happens in the years of *vanaprastha*. You can't just show up and expect to be enlightened; that would be like showing up to the Olympics without ever having trained as an athlete.

I think this is something we intuitively understand—that as we mature we should seek spiritual growth in anticipation of an old age filled with enlightenment. That is why so many are pulled to their old faith, a new faith, a deepened faith, or a renewed faith.

But some resist these changes with all their might. In raging against decline and denying the realities of change, they also block out their need for the metaphysical. They live their last decades looking out the back window of the car, anxiously watching the glorious past recede and unwilling to look into the future, with its new promises and transcendent adventures. Like the man on the plane.

I told Acharya about that man. He listened carefully and thought for a minute. "He failed to leave *grihastha*," he told me. "He was addicted to the rewards of the world." He explained that the man's self-worth was probably still derived from the memories of professional successes many years earlier, and despite his ongoing recognition, it was purely derivative of long-lost skills. Any glory today was a mere shadow of the glories of the past. Meanwhile, he completely skipped the spiritual development of *vanaprastha* and was now missing out on the bliss of *sannyasa*.

This provides a road map for those of us suffering from the principle of psychoprofessional gravitation. Say you are a hard-charging lawyer, journalist, type-A CEO, or—as I was at the time I met Acharya—president of a think tank. From early adulthood to middle age, your foot is on the gas, professionally. You seek the worldly rewards of success, you achieve some (or a lot) of them, and you may be deeply attached to these rewards. But you must be prepared to walk away from these achievements and rewards before you feel ready. The decline in your fluid intelligence is a sign that it is time not to rage, which just doubles down on your unsatisfying attachments and leads to frustration. Rather, it is time to scale up your crystallized intelligence, use your wisdom, and share it with others.

I asked Acharya what is the one piece of advice he would give men and women my age who have been workaholics and success addicts—special, not happy—and who tremble at the thought of leaving *grihastha*. He paused for a long time. "Know yourself," he finally said. "That is all. Nothing else. Nothing else can release."

"How?" I asked.

"By going within," he replied. "When your mind is quieter, you will find that treasure waiting for you within."

Faith rises as we age

Many people find that, in a midlife transitional state, their interest in religion and spirituality unexpectedly increases. Faith, religion, spirituality, or perhaps just interest in the transcendent commonly grows in our hearts as we move into middle adulthood. Perhaps this seems odd to you, because people often become more skeptical of "magical" things. Nobody over ten, let alone forty, believes in the Easter Bunny, but it is strikingly common to find religious yearnings creeping in during one's forties and fifties or later. For many, the metaphysical begins to feel *real* as we get older, and changes to ourselves are occurring that we can't explain.

The theologian James Fowler explained this pattern in his famous 1981 book, *Stages of Faith*.[2] After studying hundreds of human subjects, Fowler observed that as young adults, many people are put off by ideas that seem arbitrary or morally retrograde, such as those surrounding sexuality. They may also become disillusioned by religion's inability to explain life's hardest puzzles—for example, the idea of a loving God in the face of a world full of suffering.

As they get older, however, people begin to recognize that nothing is tidy in life. This, according to Fowler, is when they become tolerant of religion's ambiguities and inconsistencies and start to see the beauty and transcendence in faith and spirituality—either their own faith from childhood or some other. Fowler's later research asked whether the stages he found in the 1970s and 1980s held with modern developments (such as falling religious participation in the United States); he observed that they did.[3]

Strivers, however, are often the least prepared for this change, because many have made little or no investment in this area of life. On the way up, professionally, faith and spirituality might be "nice to have" but not any kind of priority, so they languish.

For those who embrace faith at this stage, however, it is a joyful epiphany. Mountains of research show that religious and spiritual adults are generally happier and generally suffer less depression than those who have no faith.[4] And the benefits of finding faith as an adult go beyond life satisfaction, according to research on the subject: religion and spirituality are also linked to better physical health.[5] This could be in part because the majority of studies find practitioners are less likely than others to abuse drugs and alcohol.[6]

Researchers sometimes halfheartedly speculate on why this is so, pointing to healthy lifestyles or increased social interaction when people attend religious services. After many years in this field, I believe these things are true, but the best explanation for the happiness bump is far simpler than these roundabout benefits. When you spend serious time and effort focused on transcendental things, it puts your little world into proper context and takes the focus off yourself. Most of our days, I am thinking *me, me, me.* It's like watching the same dreary television show, over and over, all day long. It's so *boring.* Faith forces me into the cosmos, to consider the source of truth, the origin of life, and the good of others. This focus brings refreshment and relief.

A common question I get is whether this higher focus must be religious or spiritual. Can it be, say, an interest in philosophy? To this, the answer is yes. A perfect example is the growing interest today among young people in ancient Greek thinking—specifically, Epicurean and Stoic philosophy. Many in the last few years have taken a keen interest in the works of Epicurus, Epictetus, Seneca, and Marcus Aurelius. And not for intellectual reasons—they find secrets to the meaning of their lives therein, and it brings them happiness.

The bottom line: if you are in a transitional state in your life and find your interest in the transcendental growing—even if you have marginalized this part of life in the past—you are right on schedule. Don't resist.

My faith and my guru

Religion and spirituality are touchy subjects—they are personal, and sometimes controversial. There is a reason why so many social clubs ban the discussion of politics and religion: disagreements have ended friendships and started wars. Discussions of religion are fraught with mistrust, because it often feels like someone is "trying to sell you a Buick"—to proselytize instead of giving questions and ideas fair and open treatment. I debated leaving out this chapter.

There's no real way to get around these problems completely, but it helps when your interlocutor in a conversation about faith lays her or his cards on the table. You can assess arguments better when at least you know where someone is coming from. That way, agendas are harder to hide.

In that spirit, let me tell you about my own faith journey. I am a Roman Catholic convert, having come into the church as a teenager after being raised in an observant Protestant home. My Christian faith was central to my parents' lives and it is central to my life as well, even though I practice it in a different way than they did.

My spiritual inspirations come from all over the place, from my study of other religions, to my love of mathematics, to the music of J. S. Bach, whom I profiled a few chapters ago as the sine qua non of jumping from fluid to crystallized intelligence.

I also take inspiration from Bach's faith itself. His career adaptation was not the most salient aspect of his personal story; rather, it was his relationship with God. The Bach family Bible was dog-eared from his daily reading, its margins full of his notes of thanks and praise. He finished each of his scores with the words *Soli Deo gloria*: "Glory to God alone." He believed every note he wrote was sanctified and divinely inspired: "I play the notes as they are written," he said, "but it is God who makes the music." When asked why he wrote music, his answer was simple but profound: "The aim and final end of all music should be none other than the glory of God and the refreshment of the soul."[7]

I wanted to answer like Bach about my own work—to sanctify it to the glory of God and the service of others. Indeed, this is one of the reasons I moved from music to social science, as absurd as that might sound.

My wife's path to faith was different. She was raised in ultra-secular Barcelona. (If you are thinking, "But Spain is a very religious place," your views are out of date—Spain today is effectively a post-Christian country . . . think Denmark.) She hadn't attended Mass more than a few times in her entire life. She was not religious and, in fact, pretty hostile to religions of all varieties—especially Catholicism. After marrying, I went to church, but my wife did not accompany me. When our kids were born, I took them with me on Sunday mornings while she got a break and slept in. It went on like this for a long time, and it was a source of sadness for me.

I had nearly given up on the idea that she might find her own faith when—suddenly, it seemed to me—an interest in Catholic spirituality sprang up in her. I don't really know what happened. Over the following decade, her faith grew as she practiced, studied, and learned. It became the center of her life, and she became the more religiously adept of the two of us.

And then, when I started this project several years ago, I felt a pull to inflect my own faith upward—to get more serious about what I believe. That was the motivating factor behind my sojourn into the southern Indian countryside in 2018. Acharya's lessons about *vanaprastha* greatly expanded my consciousness, connecting my spiritual journey, the crystallized intelligence curve, and chipping things away.

I told Acharya about Ester—how we met thirty years ago when I was on a chamber music tour in Europe; how I believed I fell in love after just a couple of hours, even though we didn't speak a word of the same language; how I quit my job in New York and moved to Barcelona in a bid to convince her to marry me.

Acharya asked about her faith life. I told him the truth: she came late to it, but now Ester leads me down the path of righteousness. She teaches me scripture. She helps me in my prayers. She takes me every single day to Mass. He silently contemplated this for a moment. Then he said, matter-of-factly, "She is your guru."

In the sacred Hindu text Uddhava Gita, Lord Krishna teaches, "One who desires to adopt the third order of life, *vanaprastha*, should enter the forest with a peaceful mind, leaving his wife with his mature sons." But then he adds, "Or else taking her along with him."[8]

I'll take that second option.

Nicodemus at night

Developing your spiritual life can seem daunting. Some people don't know where to start. But others, after a striver's life of self-sufficiency, are reluctant even to admit they want to try. I call this latter situation the "Nicodemus syndrome."

Nicodemus was a Pharisee, a member of the powerful group of religious leaders called the Sanhedrin in Palestine in the early years of the Common Era. He was risking a lot when he snuck out at night to an illicit meeting. But the pull on his heart was just too strong; for days he had thought about almost nothing else. The object of his attraction was not a mistress but a spiritual teacher different from any he had ever heard or met. The teacher performed signs and miracles; more to the point, he seemed to know Nicodemus intimately despite the fact that they had only just met. "Alas, how truly / He readeth what is passing in my heart!" poet Henry Wadsworth Longfellow imagines him saying.[9]

Nicodemus found the teacher on the dark street, waiting for him with an expression at once penetrating and peaceful. But he was silent: it was the Pharisee's moment to bear his soul. "Rabbi, we know that you are a teacher who has come from God," said Nicodemus. "For no one could perform the signs you are doing if God were not with him."

The teacher was, of course, Jesus of Nazareth. For months, Nicodemus's fellow Pharisees had railed against Jesus for openly flouting their rules of the sabbath and having the nerve to denounce them as hypocrites. Nicodemus should have hated him as well, but his attraction to the teacher's message of God's tender love came at a key moment in his life—a moment in which he had begun to question his long-held beliefs.

When Nicodemus shows up four chapters later in the Gospel of Saint John, we now find him in a transitional state, between his old beliefs and the new ones that attract him. He is in a group of Pharisees intent on arresting Jesus for his heretical teachings. Still on the side of the "establishment," Nicodemus nonetheless openly defends Jesus to his colleagues, asking them, "Our law does not judge people without first giving them a hearing to find out what they are doing, does it?"

Predictably, his fellow Pharisees turn on Nicodemus. "Surely you are not also from Galilee," they ask mockingly, for Jesus's home region of Galilee is a backwater compared with cosmopolitan Jerusalem; "fly-over country," you might say today. "Search and you will see that no prophet is to arise from Galilee." He is now in an awkward position. Imagine defending an unpopular Democrat at a Republican rally—or vice versa—and you get a small hint of what he must have experienced.

His defense of Jesus has imperiled his status, and being between two camps simply will not do. What does he choose? We have to wait twelve more chapters to find out, when Nicodemus shows up one last time, in the immediate aftermath of Jesus's execution on the cross. Unlike so many followers who scatter when the teacher is put to death, Nicodemus takes responsibility for Jesus's lifeless body, preserving it with "a mixture of myrrh and aloes, about seventy-five pounds." He is now clearly "all in," devoted to Jesus even after the Master's death.

Today, Nicodemus is a saint in the Catholic and Eastern Orthodox churches and, charmingly, the official patron saint of curiosity. No matter what your spiritual predilections, perhaps his transformation has lessons for you.

Overcoming obstacles in the road

The Nicodemus syndrome is just one barrier. There are others that can cause a spiritually hungry person to turn back if he or she can't see a way around them—especially if it is all brand new.

1. THE "NONE" IN THE MIRROR

Nicodemus came to Jesus at night because he didn't want anyone to witness his meeting. A powerful, successful man, he was afraid to be seen questioning his established beliefs and considering something new.

I often meet middle-aged people who are having religious stirrings for the first time, or at least for the first time since they were young. But like Nicodemus, many find these urges confusing and even troubling, especially if they always neglected faith as unimportant, or moved away from faith earlier in life and redefined themselves as non-religious—or even anti-religious. To relax this stance makes people feel like others will find them weak, or flaky.

Further, it can disequilibrate a person's self-concept, which is intensely uncomfortable. Psychologist Carl Rogers famously argued that we always need an answer to the question "Who am I?"[10] We develop our self-concept as we grow and age; Rogers defined well-balanced people as those with a self-concept that matches their life experiences. In contrast, Rogers defined a neurotic person as one who could not accept her or his own experiences as valid, and thus who has a distorted self-concept.

We resist any deviation from our self-concept because it provokes feelings of insecurity. This is why adolescence is so hard. Teenagers literally don't know the answer to the "Who am I?" question, and it makes them a little nuts. It is also why parents sometimes find them so alarmingly different when they come back home the first time from college.

Adolescence isn't the only time when self-concept becomes especially fluid; another classic self-concept crisis is when, as adults, we inexplicably begin to question our declared self as a non-religious person, or in the parlance of survey research, a "none," as a fifth of Americans classify themselves.[11] While "none" might not seem like a barrier to finding faith—it's a void to be filled, right?—it is actually a commitment, an identity as powerful as "Jew" or "Buddhist."

To change the self-concept as a "none" is confusing, and hard on one's pride. Pride freezes us in our own image, beliefs, and positions. To become unfrozen from a committed stance as a "none" can be humiliating, a declaration of weakness. I have known people who, after years declaring the stupidity of religion and spirituality, wind up sneaking off to church, as if it were some sort of illicit love affair. That's Nicodemus at night.

But even if "none" is an accurate portrayal of you at the moment, it does not have to hamstring your openness to religion and spirituality. The key is to subtly shift your self-concept from "none" to "none right now" or, perhaps, "none, but open to suggestion." This injects the element of vulnerability to your understanding of yourself, which has a powerful effect. While you may not have faith right now, the door is cracked open. Something might wander in.

2. SANTA IN THE CHURCH

Once when my kids were little, we drove past a local church, and my elder son, then about four years old, asked whether Santa Claus lived there. My wife and I found that hilarious, but it highlights a typical problem in the formation of faith: our first impression of faith and spirituality tends to be childish— and that impression can haunt us as we mature. We often dismiss religion as a mishmash of myths and childish nonsense that well-adjusted adults should logically leave behind.

Many opponents of religion attack it by appealing to these memories. For example, just before Christmas in 2010, I saw a billboard at the mouth of the Lincoln Tunnel (which takes tens of thousands of commuters from New Jersey into New York City each day) featuring the silhouette of the Three Kings approaching Bethlehem. The caption underneath read, "You KNOW It's a Myth. This Season, Celebrate REASON!"

I will admit that I broke out laughing when I saw it (even though I am a religious person) because it was such a clever ploy by a group opposed to all religion. But it was not an appeal to *reason*—exactly the contrary. It was an appeal to us to reduce faith to a Bible story many of us heard as children and reject it outright if, as adults, it does not seem likely to be literally accurate in every detail. That's about as reasonable as divorcing your spouse because he or she doesn't live up to happily-ever-after fairy tales you heard as a child. It is childish.

When spiritual urges arise, the appropriate course of action for adults is not to cross-reference them to naïve ideas we had as children—we wouldn't do that in any other area of life. Rather, it is to look to greater minds than our own. Every major religious, spiritual, and philosophical tradition boasts a library of writers and thinkers beyond what we could apprehend in a lifetime. For example, Thomas Aquinas was an unparalleled genius, reportedly writing twenty-five books at once, all of them learned and erudite. His greatest work, the magisterial *Summa Theologica*, is a masterpiece of philosophy and anticipated almost every serious objection to faith.

If you admit your view of your childhood religion was naïve, you can allow yourself to search for transcendental truths not as you first learned them, but rather from a mature, critical perspective. This requires that you emancipate yourself from the cartoon versions in your mind—leave them behind—and expose yourself with an openness to the thinking and writing of scholars and worthy practitioners.

3. THE TYRANNY OF TIME

To practice faith requires time and effort; there's no getting around this. As such, it competes with the demands of our ordinary lives. You can't really contemplate the secrets of the universe in a couple of hours; that's more like a commitment to watching a movie. If you attend worship services, right there that's a couple of hours every week. If you read, pray, or meditate—and want to get something out of it—that's time every day. And these are just table stakes. Any advanced practitioner of faith or spirituality spends as much time on this as a fitness buff does at the gym, because that's what it takes to make progress. It's also what they want to do, because it is deeply gratifying.

But at least at the beginning, it's a huge time imposition. As such, many people craving faith simply never find the time or never devote enough effort to develop anything meaningful. They just kick the can of faith down the road of life and wind up saying, as one elderly friend (who has since died) confessed to me, "My one true regret is not having gotten around to my faith."

The solution here is to stop seeing your spiritual development as a side interest but rather to put it front and center. If I told you that you had a serious health problem requiring that you exercise half an hour a day and take some medicine, you would do it. Not everyone would, but *you* would—I know this because no one reading this far into this book is a slacker about self-development. Well, your spiritual development is that important. You must make the time by scheduling your meditation, prayer, reading, and practice. Every day.

Walking into transcendence

For many, what's needed is simply an excuse to get started—a punctuation to the equilibrium of life that allows them to try something new. Here's a simple suggestion: go for a walk.

When I was with Acharya, my spiritual senses heightened, I noticed something I had not seen in my many previous trips to India: the number of people walking on the road, deep in prayer. In some places, such as the holy city of Mathura (the city believed to be the birthplace of Lord Krishna that today boasts five thousand temples), these praying walkers were everywhere. I asked an Indian friend about this tradition. "Those are *yaatrees*," he told me—pilgrims. In the Hindu tradition, the "wanderer," often a penniless mendicant, is held in reverence, and pilgrimage is considered central to spiritual awakening for ordinary people.

Nearly all major religions have pilgrimages, which are, according to different definitions, "the physical traversing of some distance from home to the holy place," motivated by sentiment or belief, and undertaken as an act of devotion.[12] from the Muslim hajj to Mecca to the Buddhists' trek to Bodh Gaya (where they find the fig tree under which the Lord Buddha is said to have obtained enlightenment). And for Catholics, there is the famous Camino de Santiago, or Way of Saint James, across northern Spain.

Since meeting Acharya, I have walked two weeklong portions of the Camino, navigating a different route each time through rural villages and over Roman roads to the famous Cathedral of Santiago de Compostela, where the remains of Saint James the Apostle (Santiago, in Spanish), are believed to be held. It has attracted millions since it was established in the ninth century. It fell into disuse in the twentieth century before becoming popular because of the 2010 movie *The Way*, starring Martin Sheen. Since then, the Camino de Santiago has seen an explosion in the number of pilgrims, rising from 145,877 in 2009 to 347,578 in 2019.[13]

Why do they do it? For one thing, walking is excellent exercise; indeed, it is one of the best exercises we can engage in for health and happiness. Some hope it will be an adventure, which is how it is aggressively marketed by the Spanish government. This perplexes me, because an adventure it is certainly *not*, unless your idea of thrill-seeking involves a monotonous, repetitive act carried out for hours a day. There is no danger besides the occasional village dog, and no huge challenge beyond the sore muscles and blisters from walking twenty kilometers per day.

The secret of the Camino is, on the contrary, the utter *lack* of thrills. At the beginning of the journey, interior shouting torments the pilgrim, who is unaccustomed to monotony and boredom. A thousand thoughts about life's exigencies bite at the ankles; one is tempted to stop at every roadside café offering Wi-Fi to check in on the outside world. But by about day three, this begins to subside as the walk begins to harmonize the mind with the body to a pace that is natural and unforced. The walk becomes a long piece of music—an *andante*, of course—which neither lags nor hurries, and thus brings a sense of ease.

The Camino is a form of extended walking meditation, a practice in many traditions. "Each mindful breath, each mindful step, reminds us that we are alive on this beautiful planet," explains the Buddhist master Thich Nhat Hanh.[14] "We don't need anything else. It is wonderful enough just to be alive, to breathe in, and to make one step." The Japanese theologian Kosuke Koyama mixes the Eastern idea with his Christian faith in his book *Three Mile an Hour God*, which refers to "the speed we walk and therefore it is the speed the love of God walks."[15]

The transcendent effects of a pilgrimage appear after a few days, in waves of perception. Indeed, my own experiences sound almost like what others say they derive from hallucinogens. For example, I enjoy rare relief from the hedonic treadmill. The Camino is all about walking, not arriving, which lays bare the satisfaction conundrum: Fulfillment cannot come when the present moment is little more than a struggle to bear in order to attain the future, because that future is destined to become nothing more than the struggle of a new present, and the glorious end state never arrives. The focus must be on the walk that is life with its string of present moments.

Each present moment, in turn, provides small satisfactions we miss when the focus is only on bigger and better. For example, one morning my wife and I spied the oddest flower we had ever seen, the blue passion flower (*Passiflora caerulea*) originally native to South America but now contentedly at home in Galicia. Alien-looking antennae sit atop threadlike tricolor petals, which bloom out of perfectly symmetrical leaves. We stared at it, transfixed, for ten minutes. This would be an impossible dalliance on a typical day commuting on the hedonic treadmill, running for prizes that pale in comparison—literally—with the blue passion flower.

The forced separation from ordinary ambitions temporarily rightsizes one's life. The Dalai Lama has often reminded me that I am "one of seven billion." By this, he does not mean that I am insignificant or just like everyone else. Rather, he is encouraging me to zoom out from my narrow, earthbound perspective on *my* life, *my* work, *my* relationships, *my* money. This is difficult ordinarily; it is easy on the Camino. As I walk, I envision myself as one of seven billion people existing briefly on a timeline lasting millions of years from the past into the future. I consider the insignificance not of my life, but of the worldly details with which I usually distract myself from metaphysical truths. I think, for example, how truly trivial it would be in the broad scheme of things if I lost my smartphone or dented my car.

While the steps mark each present moment, a day is a perfect span of time to dedicate to a different intention—to focus in prayer or meditation on the good of another. One day it is personal: my son in the Marines; another day it is global: the people of the world suffering from poverty and conflict. The walking meditation creates a sense of love and compassion for the objects of each intention, and finishes with a concrete resolution to act accordingly.

Finally, there is gratitude. Many have written about the so-called "gratitude walk," the practice of focusing on the positive events in your life while walking, helping you to savor happiness by amplifying gratitude. I practiced this all throughout the coronavirus lockdowns, around my neighborhood nightly after dinner. It was one of the sweetest memories I have of that period, and it inadvertently prepared me for my Camino in 2021. Almost the moment I began the journey, my gratitude began to bubble up—for my family, faith, friends, and work; but also for a cool drink of water, taking off my shoes, and a soft pillow at night.

I will be processing my Caminos for years to come. They helped me understand much of the change and turbulence in my own life and positioned me for a *vanaprastha* that is fruitful. Despite my best efforts here to describe them, they are fundamentally an ineffable experience, and a highly personal one as well. "It's your road and yours alone," wrote the Sufi poet Rumi.[16] "Others may walk it with you, but no one can walk it for you." All I can say is that you won't be the same afterward. It will supercharge your *vanaprastha*. You might just walk right onto your second curve.

The strength to jump

When we think of our identities as fixed and unchanging—*I am this kind of person; I am not that kind of person*—we're shutting ourselves off from many of life's possibilities. Being open to reevaluating our ideas about ourselves can keep us from getting stuck in patterns that aren't true to our changing selves. And what I have presented here shows that when it comes to faith, many people *do* change with age. Allowing that change to happen and developing our inner life helps us get onto the second curve.

What so often holds people back, as in the case of Nicodemus, is that it feels like a kind of weakness to lean on spirituality after a lifetime of holding up oneself. And if there's one thing strivers hate, it's weakness. As I have shown in this chapter, however, wanting spiritual depth is not a weakness, it is a new source of strength—strength needed to jump to the crystallized intelligence curve.

Spiritual longings are not just a special case of strengths looking like weaknesses. Our lives are full of these things, and that is the next lesson we need to learn to get on the second curve.

CHAPTER 8

Make Your Weakness Your Strength

WHO IS THE MOST SUCCESSFUL entrepreneur in human history? Henry Ford? Steve Jobs, perhaps?

For my money, that distinction, hands down, goes to Saul of Tarsus—later Saint Paul, to Christians. Even if you aren't a Christian, hear me out: He was the first-century convert to the teachings of Christ who organized the work of a messianic itinerant preacher into a body of coherent theology and spread it around the ancient world. Arguably, Paul is the inventor of Christianity as an organized religion, which has grown for two thousand years and today has more than two billion followers.

The iPhone's one billion current users isn't too shabby, I

suppose. But let's just wait and see how well it is doing in the year 4000.

So what was Paul's entrepreneurial secret? Here it is, in his own words from a letter to the start-up Christian church in Corinth in about AD 55:

> I was given a thorn in my flesh, a messenger of Satan, to torment me. Three times I pleaded with the Lord to take it away from me. But he said to me, "My grace is sufficient for you, for my power is made perfect in weakness." Therefore I will boast all the more gladly about my weaknesses, so that Christ's power may rest on me. That is why, for Christ's sake, I delight in weaknesses, in insults, in hardships, in persecutions, in difficulties. For when I am weak, then I am strong.[1]

Scholars have long speculated on what exactly Paul meant about his "thorn." Some think it was a temporary blindness, like he had suffered when famously struck down on the road to Damascus. Did this blindness return from time to time? In contrast, many medieval theologians were persuaded that Paul's torment was stigmata, a mystical phenomenon in which a person so deeply identifies with the suffering of Jesus that he or she develops the wounds of crucifixion on hands and feet.[2] Another theory is that Paul was referring to the constant persecution he suffered at the hands of the Jewish and Roman authorities. Finally, some thought he might have meant the temptations of sin.

In a more modern analysis in the *Journal of Neurology*,

neurologist David Landsborough hypothesized that Paul's torment was most likely temporal lobe epilepsy, which would explain the ecstatic personal experiences such as being "caught up to paradise," as he mentions in his letters, and seeing visions.[3] This could also explain the flash of light he experienced on the road to Damascus, followed by temporary blindness, too. This condition would have progressed through his life to more generalized convulsions, Landsborough argues, and it could most certainly have seemed like a thorn in the flesh sent by Satan.

Given the way he writes, we have to assume that most of Paul's followers in the early Christian churches knew full well the nature of his affliction; he must have talked about it openly many times and found it unnecessary here to describe it in any more detail. The real question is why he reminded them of this weakness. Was it to stimulate pity or guilt among his followers? Certainly not. His clear purpose was to show them that he—the great Paul, visionary and apostle of Christ—was flawed, mortal, and weak.

But Paul goes further: he says that this is his source of strength! This is a man whose force of will and oratorical gifts—traditional leadership strengths—brought in many thousands of converts to a brand-new religion and created the basis of its theology. Yet he was claiming his true strength was his torment and—if Landsborough was correct—his physical deterioration.

At first consideration, this seems like a leadership lesson worthy of *Through the Looking-Glass*, where up is down and backward is forward. For most of us, it sounds both impossible and insane to advertise our decline to those we need to impress.

"Hey everyone—I am sick, suffering, and getting worse! Want to join my religion?" That's pretty bad marketing. And advertising our own source of decline always seems bad for us, too, which is why people spend inordinate amounts of time and money trying to cover up the ravages of time. Botox, hair plugs, and invisible hearing aids are good business for a reason.

In the lives of strivers, no one goes around bragging that they don't have good ideas anymore, or that they lack the energy they once had. The fact that weakness and loss are bad might be the reason you picked up this book in the first place.

Decline is loss; loss is bad. Remediate it or hide it, but certainly don't talk about it! Right?

Wrong. Paul was right. The secret to going from strength to strength is to recognize that your weakness—your loss, your decline—can be a gift to you and others.

Human connection through weakness

I had a friend many years ago, a clinical psychologist with a booming practice in New England. At forty-five, he was at the top of his profession, which he adored. But he had a problem: having suffered all his life with type 1 diabetes, he was now losing his sight—not an uncommon malady for diabetics as they age. His initial reaction was total denial, and he insisted on continuing his life as he always had, including driving. He finally faced up to his impending blindness—averting potential tragedy—when his neighbors complained that he was running over their mailboxes.

He struggled for a number of years, angry at God for giving him this cruel fate. But then one day he received a phone call from a woman who told him she was experiencing a mental health crisis and needed treatment but had a reason not to divulge her identity. She was quite famous, it turned out, and desired anonymity even with her therapist. She needed—and found—a blind psychologist. He helped the woman and went on to build a practice around well-known people who desired similar treatment.

What my friend had to do was let go of his pride and become defenseless in his weakness. Only then could he prosper in a new way. This is the case made by Brené Brown in her bestselling book *Daring Greatly: How the Courage to Be Vulnerable Transforms the Way We Live, Love, Parent, and Lead*. Brown talks about making ourselves vulnerable to others if we really want to be happy and successful, that walling ourselves off hurts us. Another way to understand Brown's point is that, as we all know, defensiveness is a terrible quality and never helps us. The right goal is *defenselessness*.

But the point I'm making pushes the case a little further. It is indeed important to take risks and be willing to fail—to *dare greatly*, as Brown likes to say. But the true master then uses the inevitable failures—including the declines that inevitably follow a life of success—as a source of deep human connection.

I personally learned this quite by accident. I already told you that my college background was unorthodox, in that I got my degree by distance learning at about the age of thirty. I never really talked about this fact by the time I was an academic, because all my colleagues had gone to fancy universities and, well, I was embarrassed.

After a decade, I left university teaching to become the president of a think tank in Washington, DC—a major step in my career into an extremely high-profile position that at times was at the center of political and policy controversies. My credibility affected the success of my entire institution, so I was extremely self-conscious about everything in my background, including my nontraditional undergraduate education. In a world where it seemed like everyone went to Harvard or Princeton, I was afraid someone would hold up my résumé and say, "Hey everybody, look at this hack!"

I needn't have worried, it turned out. A few years into my tenure at the think tank, there was an effort by Microsoft's Bill Gates and a few other philanthropists to create a bachelor's degree that would cost ten thousand dollars—a so-called "10k BA." The idea was lambasted by people all over higher education as a worthless idea, because nothing like that could be any good, right? I was so enraged by this elitist attitude that I finally owned up to my own past and wrote about my ten-thousand-dollar college experience in *The New York Times*—about how my education was perfectly good, and how it gave me the opportunity to build my life and career.

I braced myself for an onslaught of derision—maybe even criticism that would threaten my position. But it didn't happen. Instead, I got hundreds of notes and emails from people who went to school nontraditionally to build their lives. They told me that it was empowering to see someone like me who shared a story not of being the golden boy with elite opportunities, but of being someone not welcome at traditional schools. I got to know and began to write about many of these people and their experiences. I became an open advocate for nontraditional education and a champion for the life entrepreneurs who pursue it.

Here is what I learned from that experience: it was through my weakness, not my strength, that I was able to connect with people I never would have met otherwise. These were strivers, outsiders who were overlooked in the traditional ways, and they were *my people*! I never would have connected to any of them had I not shared my story, with all its twists and turns.

The lesson is that if you want to make a deep human connection with someone, your strengths and worldly successes won't cut it. You need your weaknesses for that. If I had gone to a fancy college, it might impress people but it wouldn't establish a connection with most of them. "Elite" means not many have that distinction, and that distinction is hard to attain. Elite credentials don't make you relatable. They are a barrier to deep human connection.

Let's go back to Saint Paul for a moment to illustrate this. From our current perspective, it's pretty easy to see Paul as one of the great winners in history. As such, it is nearly impossible to imagine Paul as a man in decline. And yet that is almost certainly how he saw himself. Near the end of his life, Paul wrote letters from a prison cell, to churches that seemed to be fragmenting. He felt abandoned by his friends. "Demas, because he loved this world, has deserted me and has gone to Thessalonica. Crescens has gone to Galatia, and Titus to Dalmatia," he wrote to his disciple Timothy. "Alexander the metalworker did me a great deal of harm. . . . At my first defense, no one came to my support, but everyone deserted me."⁴ His only hope appeared to be in the hereafter: "The Lord will rescue me from every evil attack and will bring me safely to his heavenly kingdom." Notwithstanding his faith, Paul must have seen his earthly work as a failure, destined to be forgotten. What we see today—at least two billion Christians—would have been unimaginable to him.

No matter what your religious beliefs, there are two obvious lessons here. First, as I've been emphasizing over and over, it doesn't matter who you are—if you live long enough, you *will* see the decline of your fluid intelligence. Second, you never really know what kind of impact your work will have had. There's no telling.

But there's a more important lesson than these: it was Paul's very sadness about worldly events—while maintaining his faith—that has attracted people for thousands of years. I started the chapter by noting he connected with people through his weakness—the thorn in his flesh. But it was his words of sadness and suffering at the end of his life that magnetized the Christian faith for the ages as one of authentic human experience—a faith that understands the pain in ordinary lives and the human reaction to it.

This was not the norm in Paul's time. His philosophical contemporaries admired and followed the Stoics, who sought to banish emotional expressions of suffering from their communication.⁵ A wise person, the Stoics taught, is strong and disciplined enough to see that anger and grief are senseless and destructive. Suffering should be borne, well, *stoically.* In contrast, Paul wrote to the Corinthian church "out of great distress and anguish of heart and with many tears."[6] Paul was basically an anti-Stoic.

So ask yourself: Which type of person do *you* want to be? One who declines with seeming indifference while suffering privately? Or one who—like Paul—acknowledges loss openly and yet maintains faith, believes in the power of love, and continues to serve others?

Your decline, as painful as it is, should be experienced—and shared.

The benefits of weakness, pain, and loss

While it goes against many of our instincts, the evidence is overwhelming that defenselessness enhances life success. Studies show, for example, that when nurses are vulnerable with patients about their own lives, they are more absorbed in their work and patients become more courageous and engaged in their care, and thus have better outcomes.[7] Organizational leaders are happier—and perceived as more effective by their subordinates—when they are vulnerable and human.[8] Conversely, people who are defensive or aloof reduce trust among those they lead, are unhappier, and are less effective as a result.[9]

Vulnerability can be about little things or intensely painful personal experiences. In 2019, for example, the comedian Stephen Colbert elicited an enormous amount of public admiration when he was asked in an interview by CNN's Anderson Cooper about a plane crash that killed Colbert's father and two of his brothers when he was ten years old. Cooper had heard Colbert say previously that he had learned to "love the thing that I most wish had not happened." He asked Colbert to clarify this extraordinary statement. "It's a gift to exist, and with existence comes suffering," replied Colbert. "I don't want it to have happened . . . but if you are grateful for your life . . . then you have to be grateful for all of it. You can't pick and choose what you're grateful for."[10]

Beyond simply demonstrating incredible vulnerability, Colbert is saying that he found strength in his tragedy. The psychiatrist Victor Frankl said much the same thing in his famous book *Man's Search for Meaning*, which chronicled in intimate detail his time imprisoned by the Nazis in the Auschwitz concentration camp.[11] "When a man finds that it is his destiny to suffer, he will have to accept his suffering as his task; his single and unique task. He will have to acknowledge the fact that even in suffering he is unique and alone in the universe. No one can relieve him of his suffering or suffer in his place. His unique opportunity lies in the way in which he bears his burden." Frankl felt that people could find the meaning of their lives, and personal growth, in all kinds of suffering.

Colbert's and Frankl's ideas are at odds with the way we typically see suffering and weaknesses today—as something to be avoided, and certainly not shared. They are personal, embarrassing, or too painful to recount. Further, we have a tendency to assume that traumatic events, from accidents to illnesses to all kinds of personal loss, can only provoke pain and lingering problems, especially if we talk about them with others. However, this isn't generally the case. The key, as Colbert and Frankl suggest, is finding *meaning* in the suffering and sharing that meaning.

I have seen this remarkable transformation, and I bet you have, too. A dear friend of mine was told he would not survive more than a year after a late-stage cancer diagnosis. This was an anxious guy by nature, always stressed about life's details, and this prognosis might logically have sunk him further into his natural funk. Just the opposite happened: he realized that he had been missing his own true life and he decided that—confronted with limited time—he wasn't going to miss any more of it. He vowed to remember that every day might be his last, to live whatever life he had left simply as he truly was, focused on what he truly loved, and to share this truth with others.

By some miracle, my friend survived a year, then another, and then two decades more. His doctor said the cancer would ultimately be back at some point—the wolf is always at the door with these things—which, paradoxically perhaps, kept him from going back to his old ways of thinking. He was happy and grateful for waking up from his slumber decades ago and continued to live as if he were enjoying his last few months. When he died last year—the wolf finally got in—he was surrounded by his beloved family and at peace. He had blessed all of us with his "gift decades."

This flies in the face of a good deal of established wisdom, which has its tangled roots in Freudian psychology. Sigmund Freud believed that trauma from pain and loss is always harmful to a person, and relief requires getting beyond trauma's often-hidden mal-effects.[12] Of course, we can find many cases of deleterious trauma, including among sufferers of abuse and PTSD. But this is not the norm.[13] Emerging research shows clearly that most people are resilient—even more, that they grow from losses and negative events.[14]

Negative emotions make us more effective in our day-to-day activities. In an influential 2009 article in the journal *Psychological Review*, the evolutionary psychologists Paul W. Andrews and J. Anderson Thomson argue that sadness has persisted in the face of evolution because it brings cognitive benefits.[15] There is evidence that it makes us better at assessing reality in social situations, because we are less likely to flatter ourselves or gloss over negative truths. Sadness can even make us more productive at work by enhancing focus and helping us learn from mistakes.[16] This is how failure, via the resulting negative emotions, can help lead to later success.

Psychologists have found that many of the most meaningful experiences in life are quite painful.[17] In one 2018 study, for example, two psychologists at Western Illinois University asked a large group of college students to report the positive and negative emotions—as well as the meaningfulness—they associated with their education and with their relationships.[18] The students reported that these things gave them tremendous meaning, but that the cost was high. As the researchers summarized their findings, "Meaning involves negative affect and worry about loss."

Finally, exposure to negative emotions makes us stronger for when there is a true crisis. Research shows that *stress inoculation training*—in which people learn to cope with anger, fear, and anxiety by being exposed to stimuli that cause these feelings—is effective in creating emotional resilience.[19] It is easy to imagine that attempts to eliminate pain and weakness from daily life could lead to a sort of emotional allergy—that when hard times come and someone feels grief or fear that is impossible to ignore, that person will not have the tools to face these feelings.

Attaining greatness in weakness

"He is ready to end his life; only moral rectitude keeps him back."[20] So wrote a close friend of the great composer Ludwig van Beethoven, whose life had become a hero's journey gone wrong.

Beethoven was named after his grandfather, who lived from 1712 to 1773 and was generally considered the preeminent musician in the city of Bonn. His grandson showed the same prodigious talents from an early age: as a young man working in Vienna, Beethoven was often thought of as the artistic heir to the recently deceased Wolfgang Amadeus Mozart. He studied with the world-famous Joseph Haydn, as well as musical masters Antonio Salieri and Johann Albrechtsberger.

It was legitimate to believe that Beethoven would be the greatest composer of his time, and one of the greatest pianists to boot. Ambitious and hardworking, by his late twenties he was already famous.

For some years, however, he had been troubled by a strange buzzing and ringing in his ears. "For the last three years my hearing has grown steadily weaker," Beethoven wrote to his doctor in 1801, when he was thirty. "In the theatre I have to get very close to the orchestra to understand the performers, and ... from a distance I do not hear the high notes of the instruments and the singers' voices." He held out hope that his hearing problem could be remediated. But that hope was fading by the year, as it became clear to him and those around him that there was no hope of remission. Beethoven was going deaf.

What fate could be crueler than this? A pianist and composer can work without sight or the use of his legs. But deaf? No chance. The greatest potential performance and compositional career in a generation was disappearing before his eyes. (And while still at the height of his fluid intelligence.) It was like David striding out to battle with Goliath and getting killed in the first minute.

So Beethoven raged. For a long time after he could barely hear, he insisted on performing on the piano, with worse and worse results. He would bang the keys so hard that he ruined pianos. "In forte passages the poor deaf man pounded on the keys until the strings jangled," wrote his friend and fellow composer Ludwig Spohr. "I was deeply saddened at so hard a fate."[21]

Sounds sort of familiar, doesn't it? Have you seen someone in decline raging against it—unwilling to face the fact that his or her faculties were declining? Have you seen the equivalent of him or her wrecking pianos, to the pity of those listening?

This sounds like a sad ending for Beethoven. But, it turns out, it isn't the end of the story. He finally gave up performing as his deafness progressed but found ingenious ways to keep composing. He would gauge the timbre of notes on the piano by putting a pencil in his mouth and touching it to the soundboard while he played. When his hearing was partial, he avoided using notes with the frequencies out of the range of his hearing. In 2011, three scientists in Holland published an analysis in the *British Medical Journal* showing that high notes (above 1568 Hz) made up 80 percent of Beethoven's string quartets written in his twenties but dropped to less than 20 percent in his forties.[22]

In the last decade of Beethoven's life (he died at fifty-six), his deafness was complete, so his compositions were only in his imagination. That meant the end of his compositional career, right? Wrong. During that period, Beethoven wrote the music that would define his unique style, change music permanently, and give him a legacy as one of the greatest composers of all time.

Entirely deaf, Beethoven wrote his best string quartets (with more high notes than in works from the previous decade), his magisterial *Missa Solemnis,* and his greatest triumph of all, the Ninth Symphony. He insisted on conducting the latter piece's premier in Vienna (although there was a second conductor standing behind Beethoven whom the orchestra was actually following). After the performance, unaware of the standing ovation his masterpiece was receiving, Beethoven had to be physically turned around by one of the musicians to see the audience that was cheering for perhaps the greatest orchestral piece ever written. Being aware of Beethoven's deafness, they threw their hats and scarves in the air to make sure he could see their enthusiasm.

It seems counterintuitive, to say the least, that Beethoven became more original and brilliant as a composer in inverse proportion to his ability to hear his own—and others'—music. But maybe it isn't so surprising. As his hearing deteriorated, he was less influenced by the prevailing compositional fashions and more by the music forming inside his own head. His early work is pleasantly reminiscent of his instructor Joseph Haydn's music. Beethoven's later work became so original that he was, and is, regarded as the father of music's Romantic period. "He opened up a new world in music," said French Romantic master Hector Berlioz, who idolized the deaf composer. "Beethoven is not human."[23]

It would be naïve to think that Beethoven fully appreciated the artistic freedom his deafness granted him. I can imagine he went to his grave regretting his loss of hearing, because it cost him his beloved career as a fine pianist. He did not know the extent to which his radical new compositional style—heard only by others—would define him as truly great for hundreds of years after his death. Maybe he had a clue, however. It is significant that his Ninth Symphony closes triumphantly as the chorus sings lines from Friedrich Schiller's poem "Ode to Joy":

Joy! A spark of fire from heaven . . .
Drunk with fire we dare to enter,
Holy One, inside your shrine.

You can finally relax

To see weakness as purely negative is a mistake. Weakness befalls us all, and in many ways. It has its discomforts to be sure and entails loss. But it is also an opportunity—to connect more deeply with others; to see the sacredness in suffering; even to find new areas of growth and success. Stop hiding it, and don't resist it.

Doing so has another benefit for strivers—maybe the most important one of all: you can finally relax a little. When you are honest and humble about your weaknesses, you will be more comfortable in your own skin. When you use your weaknesses to connect with others, love in your life will grow. And finally—*finally*—you will be able to relax without worrying about being exposed as less than people think you are. To share your weakness without caring what others think is a kind of superpower.

What I am recommending here is going to be hard for some readers, though. I know, you've learned your whole life to do the opposite: show strength! Sharing weakness is hard because it is the ultimate act of subversion against your special, objectified self. You won't go down without a fight!

If you are reluctant to embrace your weaknesses, start by imagining the peace in your heart from no longer pretending you are *not* weak. Visualize others drawn to you as a person of authenticity, defenseless and unafraid. See how they relax around you and confide in you. See how it lifts their spirits to be around a person of your considerable accomplishment who is unafraid to say, "I once was better at this than I am." Imagine people who are happier and less afraid because of you. Feel the relaxation in your mind and body that comes from being truly yourself, without hiding anything, and without caring about the results. See yourself relaxing in your humility, being yourself—and thus ready to jump to the second curve.

But you still do have to jump. And as people remind me all the time, that means definitively leaving what is known and comfortable, and striking out in a new direction in life. It means a big life transition, and as we all know, transitions can be hard. So that's where we need to turn our attention next: making the jump.

CHAPTER 9

Cast into
the
Falling
Tide

WHEN I WAS A KID, I was crazy about fishing. No one in my family fished; I just took it up on my own. With money I earned on my paper route, I bought rod, reel, tackle, and books on fishing. Growing up in Seattle, I often fished in Puget Sound and, in the summers, off the rocks in the ocean in a place called Lincoln City, on the rugged Oregon coast.

Ocean fishing is fun but really different from fishing in a lake—you don't just throw in your line and expect to catch something. I learned this the first time I tried, at about age eleven. For a couple of hours, I stood casting into the water off the rocks, without a single bite. After a while, along came a wizened old fisherman from the area, who asked me how it was going.

"Lousy," I told him. "Nothing's biting."

"That's because you're doing it wrong," he told me. "You have to wait for the *falling tide*—when the tide is going out fast." It seems kind of counterintuitive, he explained, because you see the water rushing out and assume the fish would be going out to sea as well. However, this is when the plankton and bait fish are all stirred up, making the game fish crazy and looking to bite everything.[1]

Together, we watched and waited for about forty-five minutes until the tide was moving out fast. At that point, the old man said, "Let's fish!" We cast out and, sure enough, within seconds started pulling in fish, one after another. We did that for about half an hour—what fun!

Afterward, relaxing on the rocks, the old man lit a cigarette and began to wax philosophical. "Kid, there's only one mistake you can make during a falling tide," he said.

"What's that?" I asked.

"Not having your line in the water."

I have remembered that day many times while writing this book. There is a falling tide to life, the transition from fluid to crystallized intelligence. This is an intensely productive and fertile period. It is when you jump from one curve to the other; when you face your success addiction; when you chip away the inessential parts of life; when you ponder your death; when you build your relationships; when you start your *vanaprastha*.

Unfortunately, the falling tide of your life is also incredibly scary and difficult—it may even feel like some sort of midlife crisis. It might feel like everything you've worked for is rushing away. Seeing it as tragedy can be easier than seeing it as opportunity.

In this last lesson, we will learn how to cast into the falling tide—to get started on your transition—with energy and confidence. Indeed, your biggest life transition doesn't have to be a crisis or a period of loss, but rather can be an exciting adventure full of opportunities you never knew existed.

Liminality

There's nothing new about hard, scary, midlife transitions. In his fourteenth-century *Divine Comedy*, Dante Alighieri nicely sums up a fear many of us have had:

> *Midway upon the journey of our life*
> *I found myself within a forest dark*
> *For the straightforward pathway had been lost.*[2]

Psychologists have a special word for uncomfortable life transitions: "liminality."[3] It means the time between work roles, organizations, career paths, and relationship stages.

The author Bruce Feiler wrote a popular book in 2020 on liminality called *Life Is in the Transitions: Mastering Change at Any Age*.[4] He told me that he became interested in the topic after a cancer diagnosis left him in debilitating treatment and facing the real possibility of death in his forties, with young kids at home.[5] It was a period he called a "lifequake," changing his outlook on nearly everything but ultimately enriching his understanding and appreciation of his life and work. In his book, he interviews hundreds of people about their transitions, finding that a significant change in life occurs, on average, every eighteen months, and that lifequakes like his—or those that involve voluntary or involuntary career changes—happen very regularly. Most are involuntary—and thus unwelcome at the time—but nothing is more predictable than change.

Most wisdom traditions have long taught this. The Stoic philosopher Marcus Aurelius said that "the universe is transformation, life is opinion."[6] The Buddha spoke very frequently about the impermanence (in Sanskrit, *anitya*) of everything. "Impermanent truly are conditioned things, having the nature of arising and passing away," he taught. It struck him as the greatest irony that the central characteristic of the universe—change—is the thing with which we are most uncomfortable. He taught that to be at peace, we must accept the impermanence of life and existence.

There are many meditations on impermanence, and they almost all take the same basic form, of calmly noticing and accepting the change that surrounds you at every second. For example, without judgment, notice the constant changes in your thoughts and perceptions as your mind wanders from topic to topic. Feel your breathing and perhaps your pulse, and visualize the changes you cannot feel, such as the cells that are dividing and dying, the growth of your hair and fingernails. Consider the changes occurring in the world that you can't see but you know are occurring: people accomplishing things, being born and dying; the earth moving around the sun, and the moon around the earth. Impermanence is simply the state of nature.

As strange as it seems, even collective transitions on the scale of the slow-rolling, life-changing coronavirus pandemic are normal and regular, happening about once a decade. If you are my age, you remember the collapse of the Soviet Union, which radically shifted geopolitics. A decade later, you saw the 9/11 terrorist attacks that changed much about how we see the world. A few years after that was the financial crisis and deep recession that altered our economy and financial system. A decade later there was COVID-19. In the coming decade, there will almost certainly be an unwelcome cataclysmic event—we just don't know what it is yet (and it undoubtedly will catch us by surprise because we will still be thinking about the pandemic and the financial crisis).

As difficult as these are, the transitions in our private lives are harder. Liminality between the phases of adult life is especially uncomfortable because one doesn't quite know oneself anymore. As one management scholar puts it, "Employees who do not successfully traverse this period experience ongoing identity instability; they are cognitively and emotionally consumed by the loss, stagnating in their inability to let go of the old self and/or to embrace the new and changed work self."[7]

A college professor in career transition describes liminality like this:

> For almost three years now, I have been living through
> the stories I tell about being and not being there. . . .

Stories that always leave me with this sense of incompleteness. . . . I try to bridge the gap between the two places, to eradicate the distance, to stand still. . . . Standing still, trying to find my centre, me the decentred one, to find my balance with one foot on one boat and the other on another.[8]

I bet that sounds familiar to a lot of readers. It does to me, too. After a decade as president of a think tank, managing a large workforce of scholars at the vortex of the Washington, DC, policy battles, I stepped away voluntarily in the summer of 2019—an almost unheard-of move in my business. I walked away from the people and job I knew and loved and the excitement of being near the action of politics and policymaking. Why? Because I did the research in this book and committed to myself to following the implications. (How can I give *you* advice if I don't take it myself?)

This was all of my own volition, but that was scant comfort. For two years—complicated by the pandemic, of course—my wife and I were disoriented and lonely. Sometimes I woke up in the morning and mentally prepared for a day at the think tank before remembering that that was the past and that I was in Massachusetts, not Maryland. Weirdly, I noticed that my signature seemed to have changed, as if I were trying to impersonate someone else.

Liminality is uncomfortable, as all transitions are difficult. But here's the good news: even unwelcome transitions are usually seen differently in retrospect than they are in real time. Indeed, Feiler finds that 90 percent of the time, people ultimately report that their transition was a success, insofar as they made it through in one piece and with no permanent setbacks.

Even better, research shows that we tend to see important past events—even undesirable ones at the time—as net positives over time.[9] This is in part because unpleasant feelings fade more than pleasant feelings do, a phenomenon known as "fading affect bias." This may sound like a cognitive error but really isn't. Almost every transition—even the most difficult one—bears *some* positive fruit; we usually see and treasure it in the long run. For example, one of my sons is in the military. His boot camp was absolutely brutal, and a day after it finished, he told me he'd never voluntarily do anything like that again. Today, he talks about the experience—which earned him the title "U.S. Marine"—with amusement, relish, and pride.

In fact, it is the difficult, painful transitions that can yield the greatest understanding of purpose in our lives. Research on how people derive meaning has uncovered that we actually need periods of pain and struggle that make us temporarily unhappy.[10] To quote one study from 2013 that surveyed a national random sample of 397 adults, "Worry, stress, and anxiety were linked to higher meaningfulness but lower happiness."

In his book *Meanings of Life*, psychologist Roy Baumeister argues that when you find meaning, life seems more stable. Perhaps paradoxically, suffering during transitions can create the meaning in life that imposes a sense of stability over subsequent transitions.[11] This is one of the great consolations of aging and seeing a lot of change.

Even more, painful periods can stimulate intense expressive

productivity. (Remember the falling tide? That's when the fish bite.) There is a big scholarly literature on the high correlation between creative genius and mental suffering, which Sigmund Freud termed "the problem of the creative artist."[12] But you don't have to be Sylvia Plath or Vincent van Gogh to see a small version of it in your own life, as I have noticed it in mine. My comfort in exploring and expressing new ideas appears inversely proportional to my sense of stability. Among other things, this book is the fruit of my transition.

"Man was made for conflict, not for rest," Ralph Waldo Emerson wrote.[13] "In action is his power; not in his goals but in his transitions man is great." I believe this is true, but it's easy to forget. Many mornings upon waking, my first thoughts are about my old work and friendships in Washington. I rub the sleep from my eyes, get up, and cast my line into the falling tide of the new day.

Does it have to be a "crisis"?

When we hear about big changes in midlife, we often assume they are a crisis. And indeed, the "midlife crisis" has an almost mythic stature to it, especially since the 1970s, when the writer Gail Sheehy published her mega-bestselling book *Passages: Predictable Crises of Adult Life*, which sold five million copies and captured the imagination of a whole generation. Using 115 in-depth interviews with men and women, Sheehy argued that people naturally go into a midlife crisis at about the age of forty, when they question the validity of their plans and goals. What she was finding without knowing it was the anxiety people feel when their fluid intelligence is starting to decline. She, however, thought people were simply anxious about becoming old. (If age forty doesn't sound old to you, remember that the average life expectancy was around seventy back then, and people had kids so early that forty was when one's children were starting to leave home.)

Her most famous case study was that of John DeLorean, the wunderkind GM executive, who in 1969 had a great awakening. It started when he visited the retired former president of General Motors.[14] Instead of a contented, retired king of industry, he found a hollow shell of a man, sad and lonely; his life seemed purposeless and irrelevant. All he wanted to do was reminisce about the good old days when he ran the company. John saw his own future in the man and was badly shaken. "Why are you doing all this?" he asked himself afterward. "You're just like one of the machines. Suddenly you'll get obsolete and worn out, and they'll scrap you. Does that make sense?"[15] DeLorean reacted by divorcing his wife of fifteen years and marrying a twenty-year-old, divorcing her three years later to marry someone even younger. Meanwhile, he lost forty pounds, dyed his hair, got plastic surgery on his face, started writing a novel about nuclear war, and talked publicly about "neoreligious metamorphosis."

Despite all this, DeLorean comes off pretty well in Sheehy's book. But his story ended badly the following decade. He started his own eponymous car company (DeLorean Motor Company, today remembered for the car featured in the hit film *Back to the Future*). They were terribly made and very slow, promptly leading him to the edge of bankruptcy. In a last-ditch effort to raise the cash needed to keep his empire from crashing down, he turned to the drug business. In 1982, at age fifty-seven, he was busted after attempting to sell fifty-nine pounds of cocaine to a federal agent. Broken and humiliated, he became a lame national punchline. ("How can you tell a DeLorean has been on your street? The white lines are missing." Ha.) And after all that, his young wife divorced him. And you think *you're* having a bad midlife transition?

All this fed the conventional belief that midlife transitions were negative and maybe even a physical inevitability. As *The New York Times* explained in 1971, a man in midlife crisis "does not even know that something is happening inside his body, a physical change that is affecting his emotions."[16] Sheehy noted that women experience the midlife crisis as well as men, however. She herself wrote that as she entered middle age, "some intruder shook me by the psyche and shouted: Take stock! Half your life has been spent." She noted that this often coincides with early signs of menopause, leading some to wonder whether the crisis was a biological phenomenon, even in men.

Later research showed that while transitions are real and inevitable, a *crisis* is not. The term "midlife crisis" was actually coined by the psychiatrist Elliott Jaques in the early 1960s.[17] Ironically, he didn't love his own theory; according to an interview with Jaques's widow, the midlife crisis was "a tiny little early piece of work that he did" and something Jaques "didn't want to talk about after twenty or thirty years."[18] Apparently, he became unconvinced that the crisis was ubiquitous, and later research supported his skepticism. In 1995, scholars at the

University of Wisconsin published *Midlife in the United States: A National Longitudinal Study of Health and Well-Being.* Their conclusion? "Most people don't have a crisis," according to psychologist Margie Lachman, one of the project leaders. That is, most people don't have a major negative emotional event, even if they change jobs and careers.

The bottom line is that no one is doomed to turn into John DeLorean because of some temporary insanity at midlife. One thing we do know, however, is that people naturally tend to experience a big transition in the middle of adult life. We sense the decline in our fluid intelligence and that we need a change. If we know there's a crystallized intelligence curve behind it and are making a reset, we enter liminality.

It can be uncomfortable and scary, but it doesn't mean you will have a meltdown. A major inflection in your life does not mean you will abandon your spouse or buy a red sports car. On the contrary, your professional reset can bring you closer to your family and friends and inspire others.

There are famous examples of this from history. In 458 BC, Lucius Quinctius Cincinnatus was the dictator of Rome when the city was under siege. He led Rome to victory, remained in power long enough to see a return of stability, and then abruptly resigned. He retired to his small farm, where he worked and lived humbly with his family. Had he remained a dictator in Rome after his victory, he would probably today be a historical footnote—a man who governed as a dictator for a few years, gradually became ineffective and unpopular, held on as long as possible, and was assassinated. We certainly wouldn't have named a city in Ohio after him. He is remembered as great because he wasn't afraid to walk away.

I have a couple of less-famous examples that inspire me. My late father told me once about a minor mystery from his childhood. His father, born in Denver in 1893, was a Methodist minister and principal of a school on the Navajo Indian Reservation in New Mexico, where my father was born. He was beloved and successful in his job. There were no apparent problems. But one day in 1942, my grandfather (then forty-nine) abruptly announced that they would be moving. They packed up the car and headed to Chicago.

He didn't lose his job (no *push*) nor did he have a job waiting (no *pull*, either). He just had an overwhelming desire for a change. This was unusual at that time, before a job was commonly seen as a means of self-expression—a breadwinner didn't just quit his job. It was especially unusual in the middle of World War II, when the American economy was under enormous strain.

They arrived in suburban Chicago, and my grandfather showed up on the doorstep of his alma mater, Wheaton College. He asked for work. He did various administrative tasks, did them well, and over the next decade rose to the position of dean of students, in addition to teaching theology. He was awarded an honorary doctorate by the college and is still remembered fondly today by elderly alumni.

This was a major reset, but hardly a midlife crisis. The solidest of solid citizens, my grandfather never left my grandmother, never wavered in his faith, and never, ever bought a sports car. He was basically the anti-DeLorean. He simply went in search of a new adventure in which he could earn his success and serve others. And not incidentally, it was a career that amply rewarded his crystallized intelligence.

My dad never forgot his father's model of a virtuous career reset. Around the age of forty, he himself got the itch. After college and a master's degree, he had taken a dream job teaching mathematics at his own beloved alma mater. But as the years passed, my dad found he was falling behind. The younger faculty with PhDs were getting promotions and raises; he felt he was becoming a dinosaur. He thought about it for a year or so and decided to start a PhD in biostatistics, a new field for him. After four years of hard work, he published his dissertation, "An Analogue of Multiple R-Square for Uncensored Survival Data with Covariates." (It did not sell as well as Gail Sheehy's book.)

I was fourteen when my dad got his PhD. He died fairly young—midsixties—and it wasn't a happy ending. The way I choose to remember my dad is right after his career reset—proud and joyful. Here's my point: a career reset does not have to result in a midlife crisis. The trick is to be like my grandfather and father, not like John DeLorean.

Modern elders

In the times of my grandfather and father, a life reset was basically a roll-your-own proposition. No one helped anyone through liminality. Today, however, there are resources to help you. A good example is the Modern Elder Academy, started by Chip Conley.

Chip himself has a career- and life-reset story worthy of a Hollywood biopic. Worldly success came early in life—at twenty-seven he founded Joie de Vivre Hospitality, a California-based hotel and restaurant company that he ran for more than two decades. By his late forties, however, he was burned out and restless, despite the worldly success it had brought him. "I didn't want to be doing it anymore," he told me. "I felt like I was in a prison." This was compounded by a number of personal traumas, including the suicides of five close friends and a near-death experience of his own.

Chip sold his company with no plans for what to do next and wound up consulting to the start-up Airbnb, the online marketplace for temporary lodging. He thought the twenty-something founders had engaged him for his expertise in the hospitality industry but found that wasn't where his real value lay. Instead, he found himself dispensing *wisdom* more than *knowledge*—advice about life and leadership. "You are our modern elder," they told him. At first, he took umbrage at this title. He was at least two decades their senior but wasn't "old." (In California, though, youth is everything.) Little by little, however, he settled into this role and came to love the fact that sharing what he had learned in life was creating significant value.

He loved it so much, in fact, that he wanted to create this kind of opportunity for others. He knew that there were countless people his age in the phase of liminality, cognizant of the decrease in their fluid intelligence but only dimly aware of their growing crystallized intelligence. He wanted to define the modern elder role—and thus, in 2018, his Modern Elder Academy (MEA) was born.

For a week at a time, Conley brings groups of fourteen to eighteen to his small oceanside campus in Baja California.[19] With an average age of fifty-three, eight hundred participants to date have come from many walks of life—from steelworkers to doctors to retiring CEOs. What they have in common is a desire to reset their lives in a productive, joyful way in which they can serve others with their ideas and experience. There are four learning steps in becoming a "modern elder": evolve from a fixed to a growth mindset, learn openness to new things, collaborate with teams, and counsel others.

To give a flavor of the MEA program, here are questions each participant must be able to answer by the time they finish. Chip calls this "the next charter of your life," and it features a number of similarities to lessons we have learned in previous chapters.[20]

In your next phase of life . . .

What activities will you keep?
What activities will you evolve and do differently?
What activities will you let go of?
What new activities will you learn?

And to start . . .

What will you commit to doing in the next week to evolve
    into the new you?
What will you commit to doing in the next month?

What will you commit to doing within six months?

In a year, what will be the first fruits to appear as a result
of your commitments?

The first thing Chip tells participants—and it's worth re-
minding you and me—is that a reset at, say, fifty is hardly late
in life. Think about it this way: Your adult life starts at about age
twenty. If you have decent health, age fifty is most likely less
than halfway through your adult life. As I publish this book, I
am fifty-seven years old. The actuarial tables tell me that given
my lifestyle and current health (but not counting the early
death of my parents), I have a fifty-fifty chance of living *forty
more years*, and a lot of that will be working years. The point? I'm
crazy if I think it's too late to reset.

Four lessons for a good liminality

Just as I was finishing up this book, I got an email from someone I had never met, which summed up the striver's curse as
well as anything I've ever read.

> I now find myself on the wrong side of 50, with a deep,
> profound sense of regret, having spent the past 30 years
> of my life chasing one goal (work success). And while
> I've attained that goal, the personal cost has been
> extraordinarily high: the past 30 years can never be
> recovered, the relationships and other life events missed
> out on can never be experienced.

He told me he is ready for a major change in his career and life. However . . .

> I have few skills to [make a major career change. Those]
> that aren't work-related atrophied long ago. Most days I
> feel I should quit my fancy important finance job
> immediately and start over, focusing on more
> meaningful (and less time-sucking) work and
> relationships, volunteering, travel, giving my time to
> others, listening to the birds chirp, planting some
> flowers . . . but that also feels like a radical knee-jerk
> path, one which I would have no skills to navigate
> anyway.

One solid piece of advice is for him to spend a week in Baja California with Chip Conley—or attend any formal program popping up around the world to help people with their professional reset, for that matter. That's not practical for a lot of people, however. So here are some concrete lessons to get started, based on the best research and most successful strategies I have seen.

LESSON 1: IDENTIFY YOUR MARSHMALLOW

Maybe "find your marshmallow" sounds like some groovy sixties code language for dropping acid or joining a commune, but you already know that's not my advice. It's actually just a nod to a classic social-science experiment.[21]

In 1972, the Stanford University social psychologist Walter Mischel undertook a psychology experiment involving preschool kids and a bag of marshmallows. He would sit across the table from each child, take out a marshmallow, and ask, "Do you want it?" Obviously, they did. He told them it was theirs—but there was a catch. He was going to leave the room for fifteen minutes. The child could eat the marshmallow while he was gone, if he or she wanted. But when the researcher came back in, if the first marshmallow was still there, the child would get a second one.

Mischel found that a majority of the kids couldn't wait and gobbled up the marshmallow when he left the room. He followed up on the children in the study and found that those who were able to delay their gratification found greater success as they grew up: they were healthier, happier, earned more, and scored higher on their SATs than the kids who had eaten the marshmallow.[22] In the years that followed, other researchers pointed out that Mischel's results were about far more than just willpower; they also involved a child's family background, socioeconomic circumstances, and other factors.[23] But the implication remained: good things come to those who wait—and work, and sacrifice, and maybe even suffer.

The question for you is not whether you could have passed Mischel's marshmallow test; you wouldn't be bothering with this book if you couldn't, because you wouldn't have had enough success to be suffering right now. The question, at this moment of reset, is, *What exactly is the next marshmallow?* Do you know what you want as you start making new sacrifices?

If you are scratching your head, don't despair—that's what the next three lessons are for.

LESSON 2: THE WORK YOU DO HAS
TO BE THE REWARD

One of the biggest mistakes people make in their careers is to treat work primarily as a means to an end. Maybe this is what you have done throughout your career up to this point. If so, you have done what so many do on their fluid intelligence curves—have learned that's a mistake and decided it's time to stop. Whether that end is money, power, or prestige, the instrumentalization of work leads to unhappiness.

This is just one example of a broader truth, that waiting for a destination to be happy is an error. In his 1841 essay "Self-Reliance," Ralph Waldo Emerson wrote, "At home I dream that at Naples, at Rome, I can be intoxicated with beauty, and lose my sadness. I pack my trunk, embrace my friends, embark on the sea, and at last wake up in Naples, and there beside me is the stern fact, the sad self, unrelenting, identical, that I fled from."[24]

You know perfectly well that when your career is just a means to an end, the payoff—even if you get it—will be unsatisfying, because you will already be looking for the *next* payoff. If you made that mistake before, what's done is done. But don't make that mistake again. Your reset won't give you joy and fulfillment every day, of course. Some days it will feel pretty unsatisfying, like anything else in life. But with the right goals—earning your success and serving others—you can make the rest of your career itself your reward.

LESSON 3: DO THE MOST INTERESTING THING YOU CAN

Over the years, I have endured many graduation ceremonies and have observed that there are two basic types of speeches from commencement speakers. The first can be summarized as "Go find your purpose." The second is "Find work you love and you'll never work a day in your life." Which one is better advice—not just for graduates, but for all of us?

A group of German and American scholars sought to answer this question in 2017. They created what they called the "Work Passion Pursuit Questionnaire," comparing the job satisfaction of people whose primary work goal was enjoyment with those whose primary goal was finding meaning in their work.[25] Across 1,357 people in their sample, the researchers found that enjoyment seekers had less passion for their work and changed jobs more frequently than meaning seekers.

This is just an example of the age-old debate over two kinds of happiness that scholars refer to as *hedonia* and *eudaimonia*. *Hedonia* is about feeling good; *eudaimonia* is about living a purpose-filled life. In truth, we need both. *Hedonia* without *eudaimonia* devolves into empty pleasure; *eudaimonia* without *hedonia* can become dry. In the quest for the professional marshmallow, I think we should seek work that is a balance of enjoyable and meaningful.

At the nexus of enjoyable and meaningful is *interesting*. Interest is considered by many neuroscientists to be a positive primary emotion, processed in the limbic system of the brain.[26] Something that truly interests you is intensely pleasurable; it also must have meaning in order to hold your interest. Thus, "Is this work deeply interesting to me?" is a helpful litmus test of whether a new activity is your new marshmallow.

LESSON 4: A CAREER CHANGE DOESN'T HAVE TO BE A STRAIGHT LINE

We live in a culture that worships success, so much so that many of us are success addicts. Vast fortunes have accrued to tech start-up founders in their twenties, and those founders come with a certain mythology. Whether it's true or not, the entrepreneur is often depicted as having a single abiding passion for which he or she is willing to pay any personal price. Their enormous worldly rewards are portrayed as the ultimate marshmallow.

But this model doesn't describe how many—perhaps most—happy, fulfilled people have survived and thrived. Scholars at the University of Southern California have studied career patterns and come up with four broad categories.[27] The first are linear careers, which climb steadily upward, with everything building on everything else. The concept of the "corporate ladder" is a very linear one. This is also the model of the billionaire entrepreneur.

But it isn't the only career model: there are three others. Steady-state careers involve staying at one job and growing in expertise. Transitory careers are ones in which people jump from job to job or even field to field, looking for new challenges. Spiral careers, the last category, are more like a series of mini careers—people spend many years developing in a profession, then shift fields seeking not just novelty but work that builds on the skills of their previous mini careers.

So, which one is best? Earlier in your life, you might have had a super-linear career, and that's OK. But most likely, as you now move to the second curve, a spiral pattern will be more appropriate. That means thinking more about what you really want now and less about what you wanted in the past; lowering your expectations about monetary compensation; and worrying less about whether it will look to someone else like a step down in prestige or not using your past experience and skills in the most obvious way. In other words, you might just go from running a hedge fund to teaching middle school history. And that is great.

Jump

Years ago I was on a family vacation in which we were circumnavigating the Big Island of Hawaii on bikes, interspersed with sightseeing and various adventures. One afternoon we kayaked with a group of families to a rocky thirty-foot cliff called "The End of the World," from which a gang of teenagers was jumping into the surf below. One of the adults in my group said, "Anybody up for that?" Everyone else shook their heads no, so I volunteered. Looking down from the top of the volcanic cliff, it seemed like a mile to the water. My head started spinning, and I started thinking, "This is crazy, this is crazy, this is crazy."

I glanced hesitantly at a kid standing next to me who was

obviously a veteran of the jump. He grinned and said, "Don't think, dude! Just jump!" So I did. Moments later I hit the water (yes, it hurt), and it was several seconds before I popped back up to the surface. The moment my head emerged I had the sensation of being reborn.

In Tibetan Buddhism there is a concept called "bardo," which is a state of existence between death and rebirth. In *The Tibetan Book of Living and Dying*, Buddhist monk Sogyal Rinpoche describes bardo as being "like a moment when you step toward the edge of a precipice."[28] You know you have to jump to be free, but it's scary. But then you jump; there is a brief transition; you are born anew.

When I left my job as president of the think tank, it felt a little bit like facing death. It was the end of a whole style of life, set of experiences, and—I knew full well—relationships. Many readers of this book know exactly what I mean here. Perhaps you don't love your work, especially if you are past your prime and tormented. Perhaps it is like a tense marriage. Still, quitting feels like death or divorce, and before you do it, it is like standing at the edge of a cliff. You're letting go of what you have, what you've built, a professional life that answers the question "Who am I?" It is a professional death with a rebirth that is uncertain. You are looking out over a precipice, unsure whether what awaits will bring net pleasure or pain—or, most likely, both.

But you know what you have to do.

Don't think, dude. Just jump.

Seven
Words to
Remember

THIS BOOK STARTED ON an airplane at night. I asked you to
eavesdrop with me on an elderly man of great worldly accomplishment as he confessed that he'd just as soon be dead. His
abilities had declined; life had become a source of frustration
and dissatisfaction; no one cared about him like they used to,
it seemed—if they ever really did care about him in the first
place.

That experience rattled me so much that I privately started
a research agenda to see if the man's fate was inevitably mine
as well—or rather, if there was something I could do to avoid
it. I wound up making major changes in my life. I resigned
from my job and jumped into a liminal state, moved to work

that focused on my crystallized intelligence, and chipped away at my attachments. I developed my friendships and family relationships and deepened my spiritual life. I vowed not to objectify myself and to be defenseless about my weaknesses so I could truly learn my new vocation and dedicate it to lifting up others.

None of these things came easily, or even naturally. They went against my striverly urges. And this leads me to underscore once again the truth that nature is not destiny and, sometimes, we must fight our natural instincts if we want to be happy.

This is hard for some people to believe, I know. Our worldly urges for money, power, pleasure, and prestige come from our ancient limbic brains. We also instinctively want to be happy and satisfied. We then make an erroneous connection: "Since I have these urges, following them must make me happy."

But that is Mother Nature's cruel hoax. She doesn't really care either way whether you are unhappy. If you conflate intergenerational survival with well-being, that's your problem, not hers. And matters are hardly helped by Mother Nature's useful idiots in society, who propagate a popular piece of life-ruining advice: "If it feels good, do it." Unless you share existential goals with protozoa, this is often flat-out wrong.

To go from strength to strength requires learning a new set of life skills. We need to adopt a new formula, which I have laid out in detail in this book, chapter by chapter. But of course you are unlikely to memorize the last sixty thousand words. So let me summarize the whole book in seven—a formula that encapsulates all the lessons I have learned and now strive to live:

Use things.

Love people.

Worship the divine.

Don't misunderstand what I am saying here. I am not exhorting you to hate and reject the world; to live like a hermit in a Himalayan cave. There is nothing bad or shameful about the world's material abundance, and we are right to enjoy it. Material abundance is what gives us our daily bread and pulls our sisters and brothers out of poverty. It reflects the blessings of our creativity and work and can provide comfort and enjoyment to humdrum days.

The problem is not the noun *things*, but the verb *to love*. Things are to use, not to love. If you remember only one lesson from this book, it should be that love is at the epicenter of our happiness. Around the year 400, the great Saint Augustine summarized this lesson as the secret to a good life: "Love and do what you will."[1] But love is reserved for people, not things; to misplace your love is to invite frustration and futility—to get on the hedonic treadmill and set it to ultra-fast.

Take love up one level and we have worship. The writer David Foster Wallace once said, astutely, "There is no such thing as not worshipping. Everybody worships. The only choice we get is what to worship."[2] If you love things, you will strive to objectify yourself in terms of money, power, pleasure, and prestige—idols all. You will worship yourself—or, at least, a two-dimensional cutout of yourself.

Once again, this is what the world assures will bring happiness. But the world lies: idols will not make you happy, and thus you must not worship yourself. Take to heart the commands of Moses in the book of Deuteronomy when it comes to idols: "Thus shall you deal with them: you shall break down their altars and dash in pieces their pillars and chop down their Asherim and burn their carved images with fire."[3] This book showed you how. But you have to decide to do it.

The man on the plane, today

Before I finish, it occurs to me that you might be wondering, Whatever happened to the man on the plane?

He's still pretty famous, popping up on the news from time to time, although less each year. He is very old. Early on, when I saw a news story about him, I would feel a flash of something like pity—but which I now realize was really only a refracted sense of terror about my own future. "Poor guy" really meant "I'm screwed."

But as my grasp of the right formula—and the lessons in this book—has deepened, my fear has disappeared. I was thinking that I really should put him in the acknowledgments section of this book. My feeling toward him is one of gratitude for what he taught me, albeit inadvertently. He set me on a path that has changed my life. First, I did the research to expose the sources of misery among so many people who are life's "winners"—misery for which I was surely destined. Second, he set in motion a series of life changes that I never would have made otherwise. Third, I was able to enumerate the secrets to making these changes and share them with you.

In truth, the man on the plane is who I have to thank for allowing me to be happy and fulfilled for the rest of my life, whether that is two years or forty. I will go to my grave without revealing his identity. However, he will be in my thoughts every day. My hope is that before his time comes, he will find peace and joy.

And I hope you will, too.

May you go from strength to strength.

Acknowledgments

If there are errors or omissions in this book, they are mine alone. However, the work was far from a solo endeavor. My research assistant, Reece Brown, made this book possible, as did the teamwork and support of Ceci Gallogly, Candice Gayl, Molly Glaeser, and Liz Fields. These are the people around me every day working to bring the art and science of happiness to new audiences.

For inspiration and ideas, I am grateful to my colleagues at the Harvard Kennedy School and Harvard Business School, especially Len Schlesinger, who has heard me talking about this work for nearly three years and has never complained. The leadership of these great institutions—Doug Elmendorf, Nitin

Nohria, and Srikant Datar—has been unfailingly supportive of my creative work at Harvard. And the MBA students in my "Leadership and Happiness" classes were an inspiring reminder that happiness is something we can improve and share at every age.

For their encouragement and guidance throughout, I'm indebted to Bria Sandford, my editor at Portfolio; Anthony Mattero, my literary agent at Creative Artists Agency; and Jen Phillips Johnson and her team at Red Light PR.

Many of the ideas and some of the passages in this book originally appeared in my columns in *The Washington Post* in 2019 and 2020, and later in my "How to Build a Life" column at *The Atlantic*. I am grateful to my *Washington Post* editors Mark Lasswell and Fred Hiatt, and at *The Atlantic*, Rachel Gutman, Jeff Goldberg, Julie Beck, and Ena Alvarado-Esteller. Chip Conley's work inspired many ideas here. Many others—most of whom remain anonymous—contributed their personal stories to this book, which proved invaluable to me.

For their friendship and support of my work, I will always be thankful to Dan D'Aniello, Tully Friedman, Eric Schmidt, Ravenel Curry, Barre Seid, and my friends at Legatum, including Christopher Chandler, Alan McCormick, Philippa Stroud, Mark Stoleson, and Philip Vassiliou.

A number of spiritual teachers influenced this book, directly and indirectly. The first is Tenzin Gyatso, His Holiness the Dalai Lama. His mentorship over the past nine years, as well as our writing together, formed large parts of my thinking. A second is Bishop Robert Barron, who has helped me better see my life and work as apostolate. Finally, there is my wife of thirty years and counting, Ester Munt-Brooks. Through attitude and action, no one in my life has taught me more than she has about love and compassion for all people. She is my guru, and book is dedicated to her.

Notes

Introduction: The Man on the Plane Who Changed My Life

1. Bowman, James. (2013). "Herb Stein's Law." *The New Criterion*, *31*(5), 1.

Chapter 1: Your Professional Decline Is Coming (Much) Sooner Than You Think

1. Bowlby, J. (1991). *Charles Darwin: A New Life* (1st American ed.). New York: W. W. Norton, 437.
2. Taylor, P., Morin, R., Parker, K., et al. (2009). "Growing Old in America: Expectations vs. Reality." Pew Research Center's Social and Demographic Trends Project, June 29, 2009. https://www.pewresearch.org /social-trends/2009/06/29/growing-old-in-america-expectations -vs-reality.
3. The oldest peak is age thirty-nine, in the case of ultra-distance cycling. Allen, Sian V., and Hopkins, Will G. (2015). "Age of Peak

Competitive Performance of Elite Athletes: A Systematic Review."
Sports Medicine (Auckland), 45(10), 1431–41.

4. Jones, Benjamin F. (2010). "Age and Great Invention." *The Review of Economics and Statistics, 92*(1), 1–14.

5. Ortiz, M. H. (n.d.). "New York Times Bestsellers: Ages of Authors." *It's Harder Not To* (blog). http://martinhillortiz.blogspot.com/2015/05/new-york-times-bestsellers-ages-of.html.

6. Korniotis, George M., and Kumar, Alok. (2011). "Do Older Investors Make Better Investment Decisions?" *The Review of Economics and Statistics, 93*(1), 244–65.

7. Tessler, M., Shrier, I., and Steele, R. (2012). "Association Between Anesthesiologist Age and Litigation." *Anesthesiology, 116*(3), 574–79. As doctors have succeeded in keeping us alive longer, they've also kept themselves alive—and practicing clinically—longer. The *Journal of the American Medical Association* has shown a 374 percent increase in physicians sixty-five or older, from 1975 to 2013. See Dellinger, E., Pellegrini, C., and Gallagher, T. (2017). "The Aging Physician and the Medical Profession: A Review." *JAMA Surgery, 152*(10), 967–71.

8. Azoulay, Pierre, and Jones, Benjamin F. (2019). "Research: The Average Age of a Successful Startup Founder Is 45." *Harvard Business Review*, March 14, 2019. https://hbr.org/2018/07/research-the-average-age-of-a-successful-startup-founder-is-45.

9. Warr, P. (1995). "Age and Job Performance." In J. Snel and R. Cremer (eds.), *Work and Aging: A European Perspective*. London: Taylor & Francis, 309–22.

10. "Civil Service Retirement System (CSRS)." (2017). Federal Aviation Administration website, January 13, 2017. https://www.faa.gov/jobs/employment_information/benefits/csrs.

11. Adapted from Simonton, D. (1997). "Creative Productivity: A Predictive and Explanatory Model of Career Trajectories and Landmarks." *Psychological Review, 104*(1), 66–89. The curve is fitted from the equation $p(t) = 61(e^{-0.04t} - e^{-0.05t})$.

12. Tribune News Services. (2016). "World's Longest Serving Orchestra Musician, Collapses and Dies During Performance." *Chicago Tribune*, May 16, 2016. https://www.chicagotribune.com/entertainment/music/ct-jane-little-dead-20160516-story.html.

13. Reynolds, Jeremy. (2018). "Fired or Retired? What Happens to the Aging Orchestral Musician." *Pittsburgh Post-Gazette*, September 17, 2018. https://www.post-gazette.com/ae/music/2018/09/17/Orchestra-musician-retirement-age-discrimination-lawsuit-urbanski-michigan-symphony-audition-pso/stories/201808290133. One of the

few studies to look academically at peak performance among classical musicians was published in 2014 in the journal *Musicae Scientiae* and surveyed 2,536 professional musicians between the ages of twenty and sixty-nine. The researchers found that musicians themselves felt their peak performance occurred in their thirties and decline had set in by their forties. This seems to match other competitive, high-concentration fields, like chess, where top players usually peak in their thirties. See Gembris, H., and Heye, A. (2014). "Growing Older in a Symphony Orchestra: The Development of the Age-Related Self-Concept and the Self-Estimated Performance of Professional Musicians in a Lifespan Perspective." *Musicae Scientiae, 18*(4), 371–91.

14. Myers, David G., and DeWall, C. Nathan. (2009). *Exploring Psychology.* New York: Macmillan Learning, 400–401.

15. Davies, D. Roy, Matthews, Gerald, Stammers, Rob B., and Westerman, Steve J. (2013). *Human Performance: Cognition, Stress and Individual Differences.* Hoboken, NJ: Taylor & Francis, 306.

16. Kramer, A., Larish, J., and Strayer, D. (1995). "Training for Attentional Control in Dual Task Settings: A Comparison of Young and Old Adults." *Journal of Experimental Psychology: Applied, 1*(1), 50–76.

17. Ramscar, M., Hendrix, P., Shaoul, C., et al. (2014). "The Myth of Cognitive Decline: Non-Linear Dynamics of Lifelong Learning." *Topics in Cognitive Science, 6*(1), 5–42.

18. Pais, A., and Goddard, P. (1998). *Paul Dirac: The Man and His Work.* Cambridge and New York: Cambridge University Press.

19. Cave, Stephen. (2011). *Immortality: The Quest to Live Forever and How It Drives Civilization* (1st ed.). New York: Crown.

20. Imagine a simple model in which $A = \alpha P^\beta E^\gamma$, where A = agony later in life, P = professional prestige at the highest point of one's career, E = emotional attachment to that prestige, and α, β, γ are parameters. If $E > 0$, it means that prestige will increase agony. If, in addition, $\beta > 1$, A is convex in P, i.e., $\frac{\partial^2 A}{\partial P^2} > 0$, every additional unit of prestige leads to more agony down the road. Woe be unto you. QED.

21. See, for example, Gruszczyńska, Ewa, Kroemeke, Aleksandra, Knoll, Nina, et al. (2019). "Well-Being Trajectories Following Retirement: A Compensatory Role of Self-Enhancement Values in Disadvantaged Women." *Journal of Happiness Studies, 21*(7), 2309.

22. Holahan, Carole K., and Holahan, Charles J. (1999). "Being Labeled as Gifted, Self-Appraisal, and Psychological Well-Being: A Life Span Developmental Perspective." *International Journal of Aging and Human Development, 48*(3), 161–73.

Chapter 2: The Second Curve

1. Keuleers, Emmanuel, Stevens, Michaël, Mandera, Paweł, and Brysbaert, Marc. (2015). "Word Knowledge in the Crowd: Measuring Vocabulary Size and Word Prevalence in a Massive Online Experiment." *Quarterly Journal of Experimental Psychology, 68*(8), 1665–92.

2. Hartshorne, Joshua K., and Germine, Laura T. (2015). "When Does Cognitive Functioning Peak? The Asynchronous Rise and Fall of Different Cognitive Abilities Across the Life Span." *Psychological Science, 26*(4), 433–43; Vaci, N., Cocić, D., Gula, B., and Bilalić, M. (2019). "Large Data and Bayesian Modeling-Aging Curves of NBA Players." *Behavior Research Methods, 51*(4), 1544–64.

3. Much of Cattell's other work has been discredited because he was interested in eugenics and even created a quasi-religion based on it called "Beyondism." However, his two intelligences work covered here is unrelated to that and has stood the test of time.

4. Peng, Peng, Wang, Tengfei, Wang, Cuicui, and Lin, Xin. (2019). "A Meta-Analysis on the Relation Between Fluid Intelligence and Reading/Mathematics: Effects of Tasks, Age, and Social Economics Status." *Psychological Bulletin, 145*(2), 189–236.

5. Some say Raymond Cattell didn't actually invent the theory but that the real credit belongs to Donald Hebb. According to Richard Brown, "Cattell's theory of fluid and crystallized intelligence is Hebb's theory on Intelligence A and Intelligence B, given another name and popularized by Cattell. Cattell's theory was Hebb's idea." The two men actually corresponded and bickered over who deserved the credit. See Brown, Richard E. (2016). "Hebb and Cattell: The Genesis of the Theory of Fluid and Crystallized Intelligence." *Frontiers in Human Neuroscience, 10*(2016), 606.

6. Horn, J. L. (2008). "Spearman, G, Expertise, and the Nature of Human Cognitive Capability." In P. C. Kyllonen, R. D. Roberts, and L. Stankov (eds.), *Extending Intelligence: Enhancement and New Constructs.* New York: Lawrence Erlbaum Associates, 185–230.

7. Kinney, Daniel P., and Smith, Sharon P. (1992). "Age and Teaching Performance." *The Journal of Higher Education, 63*(3), 282–302.

8. Hicken, Melanie. (2013). "Professors Teach into Their Golden Years." CNN, June 17, 2013. http://money.cnn.com/2013/06/17/retirement/professors-retire/index.html.

9. Harrison, Stephen. (2008). *A Companion to Latin Literature* (1st ed.).

Blackwell Companions to the Ancient World series. Williston, VT: Wiley-Blackwell, 31.

10. Cicero, Marcus Tullius. (1913). *De Officiis* (Walter Miller, trans.). William Heinemann: London; Macmillan: New York, 127.

11. Seneca. (1928). Suasoria 6:18 (W. A. Edward, trans.). http://www.attalus .org/translate/suasoria6.html.

12. Psalm 90:12 (NASB).

13. To date, 1,128 compositions have been accounted for written by J. S. B. "The Bach-Werke-Verzeichnis." (1996). Johann Sebastian Bach Midi Page website, June 16, 1996. http://www.bachcentral.com/BWV/index.html.

14. Elie, P. (2012). *Reinventing Bach* (1st ed.). New York: Farrar, Straus and Giroux, 447.

15. C. P. E. was the fifth of Bach's children and the third of his eleven sons. He was born when his father was twenty-eight years old and named after his godfather, the composer Georg Philipp Telemann.

16. Some scholars dispute whether this truly is the point at which Bach died. The fugue was written in J. S.'s own hand, while at the end of his life his eyesight was failing, making writing difficult. But as always, all this is speculative grist for the academic mill.

17. Miles, Russell Hancock. (1962). *Johann Sebastian Bach: An Introduction to His Life and Works*. Englewood Cliffs, NJ: Prentice-Hall, 19.

Chapter 3: Kick Your Success Addiction

1. OECD. (2015). *Tackling Harmful Alcohol Use*. Paris: Organisation for Economic Cooperation and Development, 64.

2. Oates, Wayne Edward. (1971). *Confessions of a Workaholic: The Facts About Work Addiction*. New York: World Publishing.

3. Porter, Michael E., and Nohria, Nitin. (2018). "How CEOs Manage Time." *Harvard Business Review, 96*(4), 42–51; "A Brief History of the 8-hour Workday, Which Changed How Americans Work." CNBC, May 5, 2017. https://www.cnbc.com/2017/05/03/how-the-8-hour-workday -changed-how-americans-work.html.

4. Killinger, Barbara. (2006). "The Workaholic Breakdown Syndrome." In *Research Companion to Working Time and Work Addiction*. New Horizons in Management series. Cheltenham, UK: Edward Elgar, 61–88.

5. Robinson, Bryan E. (2001). "Workaholism and Family Functioning: A Profile of Familial Relationships, Psychological Outcomes, and

Research Considerations." *Contemporary Family Therapy,* 23(1), 123–35; Robinson, Bryan E., Carroll, Jane J., and Flowers, Claudia. (2001). "Marital Estrangement, Positive Affect, and Locus of Control Among Spouses of Workaholics and Spouses of Nonworkaholics: A National Study." *American Journal of Family Therapy,* 29(5), 397–410.

6. Robinson, Carroll, and Flowers. "Marital Estrangement, Positive Affect, and Locus of Control Among Spouses of Workaholics and Spouses of Nonworkaholics," 397–410; Farrell, Maureen. (2012). "So You Married a Workaholic." *Forbes,* July 19, 2012. https://www.forbes.com/2007/10/03/work-workaholics-careers-entrepreneurs-cx_mf_1004work spouse.html#63db1bb32060.

7. C.W. (2014). "Proof That You Should Get a Life." *The Economist,* December 9, 2014. https://www.economist.com/free-exchange/2014/12/09/proof-that-you-should-get-a-life.

8. Sugawara, Sho K., Tanaka, Satoshi, Okazaki, Shuntaro, et al. (2012). "Social Rewards Enhance Offline Improvements in Motor Skill." *PloS One,* 7(11), E48174.

9. Shenk, J. (2005). *Lincoln's Melancholy: How Depression Challenged a President and Fueled His Greatness.* Boston: Houghton Mifflin.

10. Gartner, J. (2005). *The Hypomanic Edge: The Link Between (a Little) Craziness and (a Lot of) Success in America.* New York: Simon & Schuster.

11. Goldman, B., Bush, P., and Klatz, R. (1984). *Death in the Locker Room: Steroids and Sports.* South Bend, IN: Icarus Press.

12. Ribeiro, Alex Dias. (2014). "Is There Life After Success?" *Wondering Fair,* August 11, 2014. https://wonderingfair.com/2014/08/11/is-there-life-after-success.

13. Papadaki, Evangelia. (2021). "Feminist Perspectives on Objectification." *The Stanford Encyclopedia of Philosophy* (Spring 2021 ed.), Edward N. Zalta (ed.). https://plato.stanford.edu/archives/spr2021/entries/feminism-objectification.

14. Marx, Karl. (1959). "Estranged Labour." In *Economic and Philosophic Manuscripts of 1844.* Moscow: Progress Publishers. https://www.marxists.org/archive/marx/works/1844/manuscripts/labour.htm.

15. Crone, Lola, Brunel, Lionel, and Auzoult, Laurent. (2021). "Validation of a Perception of Objectification in the Workplace Short Scale (POWS)." *Frontiers in Psychology* 12:651071.

16. Auzoult, Laurent, and Personnaz, Bernard. (2016). "The Role of Organizational Culture and Self-Consciousness in Self-Objectification in the Workplace." *Testing, Psychometrics, Methodology in Applied Psychology,* 23(3), 271–84.

17. Mercurio, Andrea E., and Landry, Laura J. (2008). "Self-Objectification and Well-Being: The Impact of Self-Objectification on Women's Overall Sense of Self-Worth and Life Satisfaction." *Sex Roles, 58*(7), 458–66.

18. Bell, Beth T., Cassarly, Jennifer A., and Dunbar, Lucy. (2018). "Selfie-Objectification: Self-Objectification and Positive Feedback ('Likes') Are Associated with Frequency of Posting Sexually Objectifying Self-Images on Social Media." *Body Image, 26,* 83–89.

19. Talmon, Anat, and Ginzburg, Karni. (2016). "The Nullifying Experience of Self-Objectification: The Development and Psychometric Evaluation of the Self-Objectification Scale." *Child Abuse and Neglect, 60,* 46–57; Muehlenkamp, Jennifer J., and Saris-Baglama, Renee N. (2002). "Self-Objectification and Its Psychological Outcomes for College Women." *Psychology of Women Quarterly, 26*(4), 371–79.

20. Quinn, Diane M., Kallen, Rachel W., Twenge, Jean M., and Fredrickson, Barbara L. (2006). "The Disruptive Effect of Self-Objectification on Performance." *Psychology of Women Quarterly, 30*(1), 59–64.

21. McLuhan, M. (1964). *Understanding Media: The Extensions of Man* (1st ed.). New York: McGraw-Hill.

22. Thomas Aquinas. (1920/2008). *Summa Theologica* (Fathers of the English Dominican Province, trans.; 2nd, rev. ed.). New Advent website, part 2, quest. 162, art. 1. https://www.newadvent.org/summa/3162.htm.

23. Canning, Raymond, trans. (1986). *The Rule of Saint Augustine.* Garden City, NY: Image Books, 56; Dwyer, Karen Kangas, and Davidson, Marlina M. (2012). "Is Public Speaking Really More Feared Than Death?" *Communication Research Reports, 29*(2), 99–107.

24. Croston, Glenn. (2012). "The Thing We Fear More Than Death." *Psychology Today,* November 29, 2012. https://www.psychologytoday.com/us/blog/the-real-story-risk/201211/the-thing-we-fear-more-death.

25. "2018 Norwest CEO Journey Study." (2018). Norwest Venture Partners website, August 22, 2018. https://nvp.com/ceojourneystudy/#fear-of-failure.

26. Rousseau, Jean-Jacques. (1904). *The Confessions of Jean Jacques Rousseau: Now for the First Time Completely Translated into English Without Expurgation.* Edinburgh: Oliver and Boyd, 86.

27. Schultheiss, Oliver C., and Brunstein, Joachim C. (2010). *Implicit Motives.* New York and Oxford: Oxford University Press, 30.

28. Schopenhauer, A., and Payne, E. (1974). *Parerga and Paralipomena: Short Philosophical Essays.* Oxford: Clarendon Press.

29. Lyubomirsky, Sonja, and Ross, Lee. (1997). "Hedonic Consequences

of Social Comparison." *Journal of Personality and Social Psychology,*
73(6), 1141–57.

30. Sorry to mix so many metaphors. Maybe metaphors are *my* barnacles.

Chapter 4: Start Chipping Away

1. Eastern philosophy obviously does not necessarily match modern Eastern lifestyles. There is a problem with materialism and acquisitiveness in China and India just as there is in the West.

2. *Tao Te Ching,* ch. 37.

3. Forbes, R. (2019). "My Father, Malcolm Forbes: A Never-Ending Adventure." *Forbes,* August 19, 2019. https://www.forbes.com/sites /forbesdigitalcovers/2019/08/19/my-father-malcolm-forbes-a-never -ending-adventure/?sh=4e80c42219fb.

4. Ironically, this impoverished nobody posthumously went on to become regarded as one of the greatest philosophical minds of the Western world. His writings defined church doctrine and directed Western thinking for centuries. His voluminous works are still studied today as unparalleled original masterpieces while still tied to the ancient Greek roots—he was the force responsible for bringing Aristotle from obscurity to a prominence he still holds today.

5. The theologian and Catholic bishop Robert Barron is most responsible for this formulation of Thomas's teaching. Barron, Robert E. (2011). *Catholicism: A Journey to the Heart of the Faith.* New York: Random House, 43.

6. Barron. *Catholicism,* 43.

7. I say this with sympathy and humility. My own doctoral dissertation, long forgotten by humanity, involves quantitatively modeling economic strategies for symphony orchestras. To force someone to read it is a violation of the Geneva Conventions.

8. Cannon, W. (1932). *The Wisdom of the Body.* Human Relations Collection. New York: W. W. Norton & Company.

9. Swallow, S., and Kuiper, N. (1988). "Social Comparison and Negative Self-Evaluations: An Application to Depression." *Clinical Psychology Review, 8*(1), 55–76.

10. Lyubomirsky, S. (1995). "The Hedonic Consequences of Social Comparison: Implications for Enduring Happiness and Transient Mood." *Dissertation Abstracts International: Section B, The Sciences and Engineering, 55*(10-B), 4641.

11. Kahneman, D., and Tversky, A. (1979). "Prospect Theory: An Analysis of Decision under Risk." *Econometrica*, *47*, 263–91.

12. Gill, D., and Prowse, V. (2012). "A Structural Analysis of Disappointment Aversion in a Real Effort Competition." *American Economic Review*, *102*(1), 469–503.

13. Shaffer, Howard J. (2017). "What Is Addiction?" Harvard Health website, June 20, 2017. https://www.health.harvard.edu/blog/what-is-addiction-2-2017061914490.

14. Tobler, P. (2009). "Behavioral Functions of Dopamine Neurons." In *Dopamine Handbook*. New York: Oxford University Press, ch. 6.4.

15. Gibbon, E. (1906). *The History of the Decline and Fall of the Roman Empire*. London: Oxford University Press.

16. Senior, J. (2020). "Happiness Won't Save You." *The New York Times*, November 24, 2020. https://www.nytimes.com/2020/11/24/opinion/happiness-depression-suicide-psychology.html.

17. Au-Yeung, Angel, and Jeans, David. (2020). "Tony Hsieh's American Tragedy: The Self-Destructive Last Months of the Zappos Visionary." *Forbes*, December 7, 2020. https://www.forbes.com/sites/angelauyeung/2020/12/04/tony-hsiehs-american-tragedy-the-self-destructive-last-months-of-the-zappos-visionary/?sh=64c29a0f4f22; Henry, Larry. (2020). "Tony Hsieh Death: Report Says Las Vegas Investor Threatened Self-Harm Months Before—Casino.org Caller Phones 911 Months Before Las Vegas Investor Tony Hsieh's Death in Effort to Help: Report." Casino.org website, December 19, 2020. https://www.casino.org/news/caller-phones-911-months-before-las-vegas-investor-tony-hsiehs-death-in-effort-to-help-report.

18. Cutler, Howard C. (1998). *The Art of Happiness: A Handbook for Living*. New York: Riverhead Books, 27.

19. Escrivá, Josemaría. "The Way, Poverty." Josemaría Escrivá: A Website Dedicated to the Writings of Opus Dei's Founder. http://www.escrivaworks.org/book/the_way-point-630.htm.

20. Sinek, Simon. (2009). *Start with Why*. New York: Portfolio.

21. Sullivan, J., Thornton Snider, J., Van Eijndhoven, E., et al. (2018). "The Well-Being of Long-Term Cancer Survivors." *American Journal of Managed Care*, *24*(4), 188–95.

22. Wallis, Glenn. (2004). *The Dhammapada: Verses on the Way*. New York: Modern Library, 70.

23. Voltaire, François. (2013). *Candide, Or Optimism*. London: Penguin Books Limited.

24. Hanh, Thich Nhat. (1987). *The Miracle of Mindfulness: A Manual on Meditation* (Gift ed.). Boston: Beacon Press.

25. Bowerman, Mary. (2017). "These Are the Top 10 Bucket List Items on Singles' Lists." *USA Today*, May 18, 2017. https://www.usatoday.com /story/life/nation-now/2017/05/15/these-top-10-bucket-list-items -singles-lists/319931001.

Chapter 5: Ponder Your Death

1. Becker, Ernest. (1973). *The Denial of Death*. New York: Free Press, 17.
2. "America's Top Fears 2016—Chapman University Survey of American Fears." (2016). *The Voice of Wilkinson* (blog), Chapman University, October 11, 2016. https://blogs.chapman.edu/wilkinson/2016/10/11 /americas-top-fears-2016.
3. Hoelter, Jon W., and Hoelter, Janice A. (1978). "The Relationship Between Fear of Death and Anxiety." *The Journal of Psychology*, *99*(2), 225–26.
4. Cave, Stephen. (2011). *Immortality: The Quest to Live Forever and How It Drives Civilization* (1st ed.). New York: Crown, 23.
5. Mosley, Leonard. (1985). *Disney's World: A Biography*. New York: Stein and Day, 123.
6. Laderman, G. (2000). "The Disney Way of Death." *Journal of the American Academy of Religion*, *68*(1), 27–46.
7. Barroll, J. L. (1958). "Gulliver and the Struldbruggs." *PMLA*, *73*(1), 43–50.
8. Homer. (1990). *The Iliad* (Robert Fagles, trans.). New York: Viking.
9. Marcus Aurelius. (1912). *The Thoughts of the Emperor Marcus Aurelius Antoninus* (George Long, trans.). London: Macmillan, 8.25.
10. Brooks, David. (2015). *The Road to Character*. New York: Penguin Random House.
11. Kalat, James W. (2021.) *Introduction to Psychology*. United States: Cengage Learning.
12. Böhnlein, Joscha, Altegoer, Luisa, Muck, Nina Kristin, et al. (2020). "Factors Influencing the Success of Exposure Therapy for Specific Phobia: A Systematic Review." *Neuroscience and Biobehavioral Reviews*, *108*, 796–820.
13. Goranson, Amelia, Ritter, Ryan S., Waytz, Adam, et al. (2017). "Dying Is Unexpectedly Positive." *Psychological Science*, *28*(7), 988–99.
14. Montaigne, Michel. (2004). *The Complete Essays*. London: Penguin Books Limited, 89.
15. Forster, E. M. (1999). *Howards End*. New York: Modern Library.
16. García Márquez, Gabriel. (2005). *Memories of My Melancholy Whores* (Edith Grossman, trans; 1st ed.). New York: Knopf.

Chapter 6: Cultivate Your Aspen Grove

1. Kilmer, Joyce. (1914). *Trees and Other Poems*. New York: George H. Doran Company.
2. Psalms 1:3 (King James Version).
3. Ricard, Matthieu. (2018). "The Illusion of the Self." Blog post, October 9, 2018. https://www.matthieuricard.org/en/blog/posts/the-illusion-of-the-self—2.
4. Mineo, Liz. (2018). "Good Genes Are Nice, but Joy Is Better." *Harvard Gazette*, November 26, 2018. https://news.harvard.edu/gazette/story/2017/04/over-nearly-80-years-harvard-study-has-been-showing-how-to-live-a-healthy-and-happy-life.
5. Vaillant, George E. (2002). *Aging Well: Surprising Guideposts to a Happier Life from the Landmark Harvard Study of Adult Development* (1st ed.). New York: Little, Brown, 202.
6. Vaillant, George E., and Mukamal, Kenneth. (2001). "Successful Aging." *American Journal of Psychiatry, 158*(6), 839–47.
7. Vaillant, George E. (2012). *Triumphs of Experience: The Men of the Harvard Grant Study*. Cambridge, MA: Belknap Press of Harvard University Press, 52.
8. Vaillant. *Triumphs of Experience, 50.*
9. Tillich, Paul. (1963). *The Eternal Now*. New York: Scribner.
10. Wolfe, Thomas. (1962). *The Thomas Wolfe Reader* (C. Hugh Holman, ed.). New York: Scribner.
11. Cacioppo, John T., Hawkley, Louise C., Norman, Greg J., and Berntson, Gary G. (2011). "Social Isolation." *Annals of the New York Academy of Sciences, 1231*(1), 17–22; Rokach, Ami. (2014). "Leadership and Loneliness," *International Journal of Leadership and Change, 2*(1), article 6.
12. Hertz, Noreena. (2021). *The Lonely Century: How to Restore Human Connection in a World That's Pulling Apart* (1st U.S. ed.). New York: Currency; Holt-Lunstad, J., Smith, T., Baker, M., et al. (2015). "Loneliness and Social Isolation as Risk Factors for Mortality: A Meta-Analytic Review." *Perspectives on Psychological Science, 10*(2), 227–37.
13. Murthy, Vivek Hallegere. (2020). *Together: The Healing Power of Human Connection in a Sometimes Lonely World* (1st ed.). New York: Harper Wave.
14. "The 'Loneliness Epidemic.'" (2019). U.S. Health Resources and Services Administration website, January 10, 2019. https://www.hrsa.gov/enews/past-issues/2019/january-17/loneliness-epidemic.
15. "Loneliness Is at Epidemic Levels in America." Cigna website.

https://www.cigna.com/about-us/newsroom/studies-and-reports
/combatting-loneliness.

16. Segel-Karpas, Dikla, Ayalon, Liat, and Lachman, Margie E. (2016).
"Loneliness and Depressive Symptoms: The Moderating Role of the
Transition into Retirement." *Aging and Mental Health*, 22(1), 135–40.

17. Achor, S., Kellerman, G. R., Reece, A., and Robichaux, A. (2018).
"America's Loneliest Workers, According to Research." *Harvard Business Review*, March 19, 2018, 2–6.

18. Keefe, Patrick Radden, Ioffe, Julia, Collins, Lauren, et al. (2017).
"Anthony Bourdain's Moveable Feast." *The New Yorker*, February 5, 2017.
https://www.newyorker.com/magazine/2017/02/13/anthony-bourdains
-moveable-feast.

19. Almario, Alex. (2018). "The Unfathomable Loneliness." *Medium*,
June 13, 2018. https://medium.com/@AlexAlmario/the-unfathomable
-loneliness-df909556d50d.

20. Cacioppo, John T., and Patrick, William. (2008). *Loneliness: Human Nature and the Need for Social Connection* (1st ed.). New York: W. W. Norton.

21. Schawbel, Dan. (2018). "Why Work Friendships Are Critical for Long-
Term Happiness." CNBC, November 13, 2018. https://www.cnbc.com
/2018/11/13/why-work-friendships-are-critical-for-long-term
-happiness.html. Dan is a partner and research director at Future-
Workplace.

22. Saporito, Thomas J. (2014). "It's Time to Acknowledge CEO Loneliness." *Harvard Business Review*, July 23, 2014. https://hbr.org/2012/02
/its-time-to-acknowledge-ceo-lo.

23. Fernet, Claude, Torrès, Olivier, Austin, Stéphanie, and St-Pierre,
Josée. (2016). "The Psychological Costs of Owning and Managing an
SME: Linking Job Stressors, Occupational Loneliness, Entrepreneurial Orientation, and Burnout." *Burnout Research*, 3(2), 45–53.

24. Kahneman, Daniel, Krueger, Alan B., Schkade, David A., et al. (2004).
"A Survey Method for Characterizing Daily Life Experience: The Day
Reconstruction Method." *Science*, 306(5702), 1776–80.

25. Kipnis, David. (1972). "Does Power Corrupt?" *Journal of Personality and Social Psychology*, 24(1), 33–41.

26. Mao, Hsiao-Yen. (2006). "The Relationship Between Organizational
Level and Workplace Friendship." *International Journal of Human Resource Management*, 17(10), 1819–33.

27. Cooper, Cary L., and Quick, James Campbell. (2003). "The Stress and
Loneliness of Success." *Counselling Psychology Quarterly*, 16(1), 1–7.

28. Riesman, David, Glazer, Nathan, Denney, Reuel, and Gitlin, Todd.
(2001). *The Lonely Crowd*. New Haven: Yale University Press.

29. Rokach. "Leadership and Loneliness."
30. Payne, K. K. (2018). "Charting Marriage and Divorce in the U.S.: The Adjusted Divorce Rate." National Center for Family and Marriage Research. https://doi.org/10.25035/ncfmr/adr-2008-2017; Amato, Paul R. (2010). "Research on Divorce: Continuing Trends and New Developments." *Journal of Marriage and Family, 72*(3), 650–66.
31. Waldinger, Robert J., and Schulz, Marc S. (2010). "What's Love Got to Do with It? Social Functioning, Perceived Health, and Daily Happiness in Married Octogenarians." *Psychology and Aging, 25*(2), 422–31.
32. Finkel, E. J., Burnette, J. L., and Scissors, L. E. (2007). "Vengefully Ever After: Destiny Beliefs, State Attachment Anxiety, and Forgiveness." *Journal of Personality and Social Psychology, 92*(5), 871–86.
33. Aron, Arthur, Fisher, Helen, Mashek, Debra J., et al. (2005). "Reward, Motivation, and Emotion Systems Associated with Early-Stage Intense Romantic Love." *Journal of Neurophysiology, 94*(1), 327–37.
34. Kim, Jungsik, and Hatfield, Elaine. (2004). "Love Types and Subjective Well-Being: A Cross-Cultural Study." *Social Behavior and Personality, 32*(2), 173–82.
35. "Companionate Love" (2016). Psychology. IResearchNet website, January 23, 2016. http://psychology.iresearchnet.com/social-psychology/interpersonal-relationships/companionate-love.
36. Grover, Shawn, and Helliwell, John F. (2019). "How's Life at Home? New Evidence on Marriage and the Set Point for Happiness." *Journal of Happiness Studies, 20*(2), 373–90.
37. "Coolidge Effect." (n.d.). Oxford Reference website. https://www.oxfordreference.com/view/10.1093/oi/authority.20110803095637122.
38. Blanchflower, D. G., and Oswald, A. J. (2004). "Money, Sex and Happiness: An Empirical Study." *Scandinavian Journal of Economics, 106*, 393–415.
39. Birditt, Kira S., and Antonucci, Toni C. (2007). "Relationship Quality Profiles and Well-Being Among Married Adults." *Journal of Family Psychology, 21*(4), 595–604.
40. Adams, Rebecca G. (1988). "Which Comes First: Poor Psychological Well-Being or Decreased Friendship Activity?" *Activities, Adaptation, and Aging, 12*(1–2), 27–41.
41. Dykstra, P. A., and de Jong Gierveld, J. (2004). "Gender and Marital-History Differences in Emotional and Social Loneliness among Dutch Older Adults." *Canadian Journal on Aging, 23*, 141–55.
42. Pinquart, M., and Sorensen, S. (2000). "Influences of Socioeconomic Status, Social Network, and Competence on Subjective Well-Being in Later Life: A Meta-Analysis." *Psychology and Aging, 15*, 187–224.

43. Fiori, Katherine L., and Denckla, Christy A. (2015). "Friendship and Happiness Among Middle-Aged Adults." In Melikşah Demir (ed.), *Friendship and Happiness*. Dordrecht: Springer Netherlands, 137–54.

44. Cigna. (2018). *2018 Cigna U.S. Loneliness Index*. Cigna website, Studies and Reports, May 1, 2018. https://www.multivu.com/players/English /8294451-cigna-us-loneliness-survey/docs/IndexReport _1524069371598-173525450.pdf.

45. Leavy, R. L. (1983). "Social Support and Psychological Disorder: A Review." *Journal of Community Psychology, 11*(1), 3–21.

46. Leavy. "Social Support and Psychological Disorder: A Review," 3–21.

47. Cohen, S. (1988). "Psychosocial Models of the Role of Social Support in the Etiology of Physical Disease." *Health Psychology, 7*, 269–97; House, J. S., Landis, K. R., and Umberson, D. (1988). "Social Relationships and Health." *Science, 241*(4865), 540–45.

48. Carstensen, Laura L., Isaacowitz, Derek M., and Charles, Susan T. (1999). "Taking Time Seriously." *The American Psychologist, 54*(3), 165–81.

49. Golding, Barry, ed. (2015). *The Men's Shed Movement: The Company of Men*. Champaign, IL: Common Ground Publishing.

50. Fallik, Dawn. (2018). "What to Do About Lonely Older Men? Put Them to Work." *The Washington Post*, June 24, 2018. https://www.washington post.com/national/health-science/what-to-do-about-lonely-older -men-put-them-to-work/2018/06/22/0c07efc8-53ab-11e8-a551-5b64 8abe29ef_story.html.

51. Christensen, Clayton M., Dillon, Karen, and Allworth, James. (2012). *How Will You Measure Your Life?* (1st ed.). New York: Harper Business.

52. Niemiec, C., Ryan, R., and Deci, E. (2009). "The Path Taken: Consequences of Attaining Intrinsic and Extrinsic Aspirations in Post-College Life." *Journal of Research in Personality, 43*(3), 291–306.

53. Thoreau, H., Sanborn, F., Scudder, H., Blake, H., and Emerson, R. (1894). *The Writings of Henry David Thoreau: With Bibliographical Introductions and Full Indexes. In ten volumes* (Riverside ed., vol. 7). Boston and New York: Houghton Mifflin, 42–43.

Chapter 7: Start Your *Vanaprastha*

1. In Sanskrit: वनप्रस्थ.

2. Fowler, James W. (1981). *Stages of Faith: The Psychology of Human Development and the Quest for Meaning* (1st ed.). San Francisco: Harper & Row.

3. Fowler, James W. (2001). "Faith Development Theory and the Postmodern Challenges." *International Journal for the Psychology of Religion*, *11*(3), 159–72; Jones, J. M. (2020). "U.S. Church Membership Down Sharply in Past Two Decades." Gallup, November 23, 2020. https://news.gallup.com/poll/248837/church-membership-down-sharply-past-two-decades.aspx.

4. Marshall, J. (2020). "Are Religious People Happier, Healthier? Our New Global Study Explores This Question." Pew Research Center website. https://www.pewresearch.org/fact-tank/2019/01/31/are-religious-people-happier-healthier-our-new-global-study-explores-this-question/; McCullough, Michael E., and Larson, David B. (1999). "Religion and Depression: A Review of the Literature." *Twin Research, 2*(2), 126–36.

5. Miller, W. R., and Thoresen, C. E. (1999). "Spirituality and Health." In W. R. Miller (ed.), *Integrating Spirituality into Treatment: Resources for Practitioners*. Washington, DC: American Psychological Association, 3–18.

6. Koenig, Harold G. (2016). "Religion and Medicine II: Religion, Mental Health, and Related Behaviors." *International Journal of Psychiatry in Medicine, 31*(1), 97–109.

7. Gardiner, J. (2013). *Bach: Music in the Castle of Heaven* (1st U.S. ed.). New York: Knopf, 126.

8. Saraswati, Ambikananda. (2002). *The Uddhava Gita*. Berkeley, CA: Seastone.

9. Longfellow, Henry Wadsworth. (1922). *The Complete Poetical Works of Henry Wadsworth Longfellow*. Boston and New York: Houghton Mifflin, 492.

10. Koch, S., ed. (1959). *Psychology: A Study of a Science: Vol. 3. Formulations of the Person and the Social Context*. New York: McGraw-Hill.

11. Pew Research. (2020). "'Nones' on the Rise." https://www.pewforum.org/2012/10/09/nones-on-the-rise.

12. Scriven, Richard. (2014). "Geographies of Pilgrimage: Meaningful Movements and Embodied Mobilities." *Geography Compass*, 8(4), 249–61.

13. Santiago de Compostela Pilgrim Office (n.d.). "Statistical Report—2019." https://oficinadelperegrino.com/estadisticas.

14. Hahn, T. N., and Lion's Roar. (2019). *Thich Nhat Hanh on Walking Meditation*. Lion's Roar. https://www.lionsroar.com/how-to-meditate-thich-nhat-hanh-on-walking-meditation.

15. Koyama, Kosuke. (1980). *Three Mile an Hour God*. Maryknoll, NY: Orbis Books.
16. Akṣapāda. (2019). *The Analects of Rumi*. Self-published, 82.

Chapter 8: Make Your Weakness Your Strength

1. 2 Corinthians 12:7–10 (NASB).
2. The most famous case of stigmata is that of Padre Pio, also known as Saint Pio of Pietrelcina, the twentieth-century Catholic mystic who bore the stigmata for most of his life. People who believe Paul suffered stigmata point to Galatians 6:17, where he writes, "I bear the marks of Jesus on my body."
3. Landsborough, D. (1987). "St. Paul and Temporal Lobe Epilepsy." *Journal of Neurology, Neurosurgery and Psychiatry, 50*(6), 659–64.
4. 2 Timothy 4:10–16 (NASB).
5. Welborn, L. (2011). "Paul and Pain: Paul's Emotional Therapy in 2 Corinthians 1.1–2.13; 7.5–16 in the Context of Ancient Psychagogic Literature." *New Testament Studies, 57*(4), 547–70.
6. 2 Corinthians 2:4 (NASB).
7. Thorup, C. B., Rundqvist, E., Roberts, C., and Delmar, C. (2012). "Care as a Matter of Courage: Vulnerability, Suffering and Ethical Formation in Nursing Care." *Scandinavian Journal of Caring Sciences, 26*(3), 427–35.
8. Lopez, Stephanie O. (2018). "Vulnerability in Leadership: The Power of the Courage to Descend." *Industrial-Organizational Psychology Dissertations*, 16.
9. Peck, Edward W. D. (1998). "Leadership and Defensive Communication: A Grounded Theory Study of Leadership Reaction to Defensive Communication." Dissertation, University of British Columbia. http://dx.doi.org/10.14288/1.0053974.
10. Fitzpatrick, Kevin. (2019). "Stephen Colbert's Outlook on Grief Moved Anderson Cooper to Tears." *Vanity Fair*, August 16, 2019. https://www.vanityfair.com/hollywood/2019/08/colbert-anderson-cooper-father-grief-tears.
11. Frankl, V. (1992). *Man's Search for Meaning: An Introduction to Logotherapy* (4th ed.). Boston: Beacon Press.
12. Freud, S. (1922). "Mourning and Melancholia." *The Journal of Nervous and Mental Disease, 56*(5), 543–45.
13. Bonanno, G. (2004). "Loss, Trauma, and Human Resilience." *American Psychologist, 59*(1), 20–28.

14. Helgeson, V., Reynolds, K., and Tomich, P. (2006). "A Meta-Analytic Review of Benefit Finding and Growth." *Journal of Consulting and Clinical Psychology, 74*(5), 797–816.

15. Andrews, Paul W., and Thomson, J. Anderson. (2009). "The Bright Side of Being Blue." *Psychological Review, 116*(3), 620–54. https://doi .org/10.1037/a0016242.

16. University of Alberta. (2001). "Sad Workers May Make Better Workers." *ScienceDaily,* June 14, 2001. www.sciencedaily.com/releases /2001/06/010612065304.htm.

17. Baumeister, Roy F., Vohs, Kathleen D., Aaker, Jennifer L., and Garbinsky, Emily N. (2013). "Some Key Differences Between a Happy Life and a Meaningful Life." *The Journal of Positive Psychology, 8*(6), 505–16.

18. Lane, David J., and Mathes, Eugene W. (2018). "The Pros and Cons of Having a Meaningful Life." *Personality and Individual Differences, 120,* 13–16.

19. Saunders, T., Driskell, J. E., Johnston, J. H., and Salas, E. (1996). "The Effect of Stress Inoculation Training on Anxiety and Performance." *Journal of Occupational Health Psychology, 1*(2), 170–86.

20. McCabe, B. (2004). "Beethoven's Deafness." *Annals of Otology, Rhinology and Laryngology, 113*(7), 511–25.

21. Saccenti, E., Smilde, A., and Saris, W. (2011). "Beethoven's Deafness and His Three Styles." *BMJ, 343*(7837), D7589.

22. Saccenti, Smilde, and Saris. "Beethoven's Deafness and His Three Styles," D7589.

23. Austin, Michael. (2003). "Berlioz and Beethoven." The Hector Berlioz website, January 12, 2003. http://www.hberlioz.com/Predecessors /beethoven.htm.

Chapter 9: Cast into the Falling Tide

1. Blauw, A., Benincà, E., Laane, R., et al. (2012). "Dancing with the Tides: Fluctuations of Coastal Phytoplankton Orchestrated by Different Oscillatory Modes of the Tidal Cycle." *PLoS One 7*(11), E49319.

2. Dante Alighieri. (1995). *The Divine Comedy* (A. Mandelbaum, trans.). London: David Campbell.

3. Ibarra, H., and Obodaru, O. (2016). "Betwixt and Between Identities: Liminal Experience in Contemporary Careers." *Research in Organizational Behavior, 36,* 47–64.

4. Feiler, B. (2020). *Life Is in the Transitions.* New York: Penguin Books.

5. Brooks, Arthur (host). (2020). "Managing Transitions in Life." In *The*

Art of Happiness with Arthur Brooks, Apple Podcasts, August 4, 2020. https://podcasts.apple.com/us/podcast/managing-transitions-in-life /id1505581039?i=1000487081784.

6. Hammond, M., and Clay, D. (2006). *Meditations.* London: Penguin Books Limited, 24.

7. Conroy, S., and O'Leary-Kelly, A. (2014). "Letting Go and Moving On: Work-Related Identity Loss and Recovery." *The Academy of Management Review, 39*(1), 67–87.

8. Ibarra and Obodaru. "Betwixt and Between Identities," 47–64.

9. Walker, W. Richard, Skowronski, John J., and Thompson, Charles P. (2003). "Life Is Pleasant-and Memory Helps to Keep It That Way." *Review of General Psychology, 7*(2), 203–10.

10. Baumeister, Roy F., Vohs, Kathleen D., Aaker, Jennifer L., and Garbinsky, Emily N. (2013). "Some Key Differences Between a Happy Life and a Meaningful Life." *The Journal of Positive Psychology, 8*(6), 505–16.

11. Baumeister, R. (1991). *Meanings of Life.* New York: Guilford Press.

12. Andreasen, N. C. (2008). "The Relationship Between Creativity and Mood Disorders." *Dialogues in Clinical Neuroscience, 10*(2), 251–55; Garcia, E. E. (2004). "Rachmaninoff and Scriabin: Creativity and Suffering in Talent and Genius." *The Psychoanalytic Review, 91*(3), 423–42.

13. Emerson, R. W. (2001). *The Later Lectures of Ralph Waldo Emerson, 1843–1871: Vol. 1. 1843–1854* (R. A. Bosco and J. Myerson, eds.). Athens: University of Georgia Press; Oxford Scholarly Editions Online (2018). doi:10.1093/actrade/9780820334622.book.1.

14. Sheehy, G. (1976). *Passages: Predictable Crises of Adult Life* (1st ed.). New York: Dutton.

15. Sheehy, *Passages,* 400.

16. Cook, Joan. (1971). "The Male Menopause: For Some, There's 'a Sense of Panic,'" *The New York Times,* April 5, 1971. https://www.nytimes .com/1971/04/05/archives/the-male-menopause-for-some-theres-a -sense-of-panic.html.

17. Jaques, E. (1965). "Death and the Mid-Life Crisis." *The International Journal of Psychoanalysis, 46*(4), 502–14.

18. Druckerman, Pamela. (2018). "How the Midlife Crisis Came to Be." *The Atlantic,* May 29, 2018. https://www.theatlantic.com/family/arch ive/2018/05/the-invention-of-the-midlife-crisis/561203.

19. Modern Elder Academy. https://www.modernelderacademy.com.

20. Used by permission.

21. Mischel, W., Ebbesen, E., and Raskoff Zeiss, A. (1972). "Cognitive and Attentional Mechanisms in Delay of Gratification." *Journal of Personality and Social Psychology, 21*(2), 204–18.

22. Mischel, Ebbesen, and Raskoff Zeiss. "Cognitive and Attentional Mechanisms in Delay of Gratification," 204–18.

23. Urist, Jacoba. (2014). "What the Marshmallow Test Really Teaches About Self-Control." *The Atlantic*, September 24, 2014. https://www .theatlantic.com/health/archive/2014/09/what-the-marshmallow -test-really-teaches-about-self-control/380673.

24. Emerson, R. (1979). *The Collected Works of Ralph Waldo Emerson: Vol. 2. Essays: First Series* (J. Carr, A. Ferguson, and J. Slater, eds.). Cambridge, MA: Belknap Press of Harvard University Press.

25. Jachimowicz, Jon, To, Christopher, Menges, Jochen, and Akinola, Modupe. (2017). "Igniting Passion from Within: How Lay Beliefs Guide the Pursuit of Work Passion and Influence Turnover." PsyArXiv, December 7, 2017. doi:10.31234/osf.io/qj6y9.

26. Izard, C. (n.d.). "Emotion Theory and Research: Highlights, Unanswered Questions, and Emerging Issues." *Annual Review of Psychology, 60*(1), 1–25.

27. Patz, Alan L., Milliman, John, and Driver, Michael John. (1991). "Career Concepts and Total Enterprise Simulation Performance." *Developments in Business Simulation & Experiential Exercises*, 18.

28. Gaffney, P., and Harvey, A. (1992). *The Tibetan Book of Living and Dying* (1st ed.). San Francisco: HarperSanFrancisco.

Conclusion: Seven Words to Remember

1. Graves, Dan. "Augustine's Love Sermon." Christian History Institute website. https://christianhistoryinstitute.org/study/module/augustine.

2. Wallace, David Foster. (2009). *This Is Water: Some Thoughts, Delivered on a Significant Occasion, About Living a Compassionate Life* (1st ed.). New York: Little, Brown.

3. Deuteronomy 7:5 (NASB).

Index